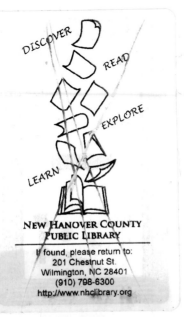

ALSO BY BRET EASTON ELLIS

Imperial Bedrooms

Lunar Park

Glamorama

The Informers

American Psycho

The Rules of Attraction

Less Than Zero

WHITE

WHITE

BRET EASTON ELLIS

ALFRED A. KNOPF · NEW YORK · 2019

THIS IS A BORZOI BOOK PUBLISHED BY ALFRED A. KNOPF

www.aaknopf.com

Knopf, Borzoi Books, and the colophon are registered trademarks of Penguin Random House LLC.

Grateful acknowledgment is made to Farrar, Straus and Giroux, and Janklow & Nesbit Associates, for permission to reprint an excerpt from "The White Album," from *The White Album* by Joan Didion. Reprinted by permission of Farrar, Straus and Giroux and Janklow & Nesbit Associates.

Library of Congress Cataloging-in-Publication Data
Names: Ellis, Bret Easton, author.
Title: White / by Bret Easton Ellis.
Description: New York : Alfred A. Knopf, 2019. | "This is a Borzoi book published by Alfred A. Knopf."
Identifiers: LCCN 2018050947 (print) | LCCN 2018055342 (ebook) | ISBN 9780525656319 (ebook) | ISBN 9780525656302 (hardcover) | ISBN 9781524711566 (open market)
Subjects: LCSH: American essays—21st century.
Classification: LCC PS3555.L5937 (ebook) | LCC PS3555.L5937 W48 2019 (print) | DDC 814/.54—dc23
LC record available at https://lccn.loc.gov/2018050947

Jacket design by Chip Kidd

Manufactured in the United States of America
First Edition

FOR MATTHEW SPECKTOR

Society mediates between the extremes of, on the one hand, intolerably strict morality and, on the other, dangerously anarchic permissiveness through an unspoken agreement whereby we are given leave to bend the rules of the strictest morality, provided we do so quietly and discreetly. Hypocrisy is the grease that keeps society functioning in an agreeable way.

JANET MALCOLM, *The Journalist and the Murderer*

Somewhere in the last few years—and I can't pinpoint exactly when—a vague yet almost overwhelming and irrational annoyance started tearing through me maybe up to a dozen times a day. This annoyance was over things so seemingly minor, so out of my usual field of reference, that I was surprised by how I had to take a deep breath to dismantle this disgust and frustration that was all due to the foolishness of other people: adults, acquaintances and strangers on social media who offered up their rash opinions and judgments, their mindless preoccupations, always with an unwavering certitude that they were right. A toxic attitude seemed to drift off every post or comment or tweet whether it was actually there or not. This anger was new, something I'd never experienced before—and it was tied in with an anxiousness, an oppression I felt whenever I ventured online, a sense that I was going to somehow make a mistake instead of simply offering an opinion or make a joke or criticize someone or something. This idea would have been unthinkable ten years earlier—that an opinion could become something wrong—but in an infuriated, polarized society people were blocked because of these opinions, and unfollowed because they were perceived in ways that might be inaccurate. The fearful began to instantly see the entire humanity of an individual in a cheeky, offensive tweet and were outraged; people were attacked 1 *and unfriended for backing the "wrong" candidate or having the "wrong" opinion or for simply stating the "wrong" belief. It was as if no one could differentiate between a living person and a string of words hastily typed out on a black sapphire screen. The culture at large seemed to encourage discourse but social media had become a trap, and what it really wanted to do was shut down the individual. What often activated my stress was that other people were always angry about everything, presenting themselves as enraged by opinions that I believed in and liked or thought were simply innocuous. My pushback against all of this forced me to confront a degraded fantasy of myself—an actor, as someone I never thought existed—and this, in turn, became a constant reminder of my failings. And what was worse: this anger could become addictive to the point where I just gave up and sat there exhausted, mute with stress. But ultimately silence and submission were what the machine wanted.*

The idea of beginning a new novel started whispering to me sometime in the first weeks of 2013, while I was stuck on the I-10 in traffic merging into Hollywood after I had just spent a week in Palm Springs with a friend I'd gone to college with in the 1980s, and who was now losing her mind. (She had broken down in front of me several times during those days in the house on Azure Court, before leaving earlier than expected to attend a Deepak Chopra retreat in San Diego. And, yes, I know how this sounds.) In Palm Springs I was unexpectedly crippled with waves of anxiety that kept me in bed for hours staring at my phone—vague yet vast realizations about mortality that my friend's frailties had activated and encouraged—while also, absurdly, furiously going through the last demented round of notes on a pilot I was writing for the CW Network. Between the bouts of fear and the never-ending phone calls from the production company and the rewrites, the thought that I might never write another novel announced itself more loudly than it had in years—and my last novel had been completed in 2009. Why this idea asserted itself at this particular time I can't tell you. The desire to write prose had kept pulsing faintly within me for years but not within what I now saw as the fake enclave of the novel. In fact I'd been wrestling away from the idea of "the novel" for more than a decade, as evident in the last two books I published: one was a mock memoir wrapped within a horror novel, and the other was a condensed autobiographical noir I pushed through painfully during a midlife crisis, a story about my first three years back in Los Angeles futilely working on movies after I'd lived in New York for almost two decades.

For those past five years I had no desire to write a novel and had convinced myself I didn't want to be constrained by a form that didn't interest me anymore. (And yet I was willing to be constrained by the conventions of the hundred-page screenplay that would never be made and the five-act TV pilot that would never be shot.) I had reiterated all of this firmly in interviews I'd given over that period, during the world tour for that last novel I'd written, at press junkets in Spain, in Copenhagen, in Melbourne. But out in the desert that feeling evaporated, and between the notes calls and the fear tamped down by Xanax and tequila, as the mountains surrounding the house darkened beneath the late-afternoon winter skies, the first paragraph of a novel began to take shape. It started with an image revolving around the bone-white Emser Tile sign situated on a rooftop at the intersection of Santa Monica Boulevard and Holloway Drive: the view from behind the windshield of a stolen car, a violent accident, an unfolding mystery, something about the past, that last year in high school, intimations of a murder disguised as a suicide, somebody pretending to be somebody he wasn't, an actor.

■ ■ ■

I've never forced a novel, something my agent and publishers and readers might think is part of an overall problem with me as a writer, or as a brand, namely because I've gone five or seven or eight years between books at a time when most people still expect a brand-name novelist to publish every other year like clockwork. This was what my publishing house had expected of me in the 1980s after my first novel was a success, and I still remember my shock at being told this. In the end I never worked like that, and yet this didn't ever mean I wasn't writing. It meant only that I wrote in a way that simply worked best for me. I wasn't thinking about anyone else when I wrote—I wasn't aware of an audience waiting for me outside my apartment, and I never really cared what my agent or editor or publisher expected from me. With my publisher I made sure deadlines (if any) were flexible (and they were), and in return I agreed to publicize the books as much as the publisher required me to. And I never succumbed to the temptation to give an audience what I thought they might have wanted: I was the audience and I was writing to satisfy myself, and to relieve myself from pain. I rarely gave interviews between book publications because part of the process was still mysterious to readers, with a kind of secret glamour that added to the excitement with which books were once received, whether negatively or positively.

But novels don't engage with the public on that level anymore. I'd wistfully noticed the overall lack of enthusiasm for the big American literary novels the autumn before I met that friend in Palm Springs, but I also realized that's nothing to worry about. It's only a fact, just as the notion of the great American studio movie or the great American band has become a smaller, narrower idea. Everything has been degraded by what the sensory overload and the supposed freedom-of-choice technology has brought to us, and, in short, by the democratization of the arts. I started feeling the need to work my way through this transition—to move from the analog world in which I used to write and publish novels into the digital world we live in now (through podcasting, creating a web series, engaging on social media) even though I never thought there was any correlation between the two. After that week in the desert with the friend I've known for thirty years, after I'd seen her driven mad by her life while I endured the endless rewrites of a sci-fi pilot that was never going to happen, something in me finally cracked and I began making notes for a novel in that last week of January. But it has never turned into anything either.

e m p i r e

I was unusually attracted to horror movies as a kid growing up in the San Fernando Valley of the 1970s, when they spoke to me in a way nothing else seemed to. I might have known one or two believers who loved them as well, but for the majority of my friends in that movie-mad decade, horror was just another genre, no more meaningful to them than the teen sex comedy or the disco musical. But what was it about horror movies—and horror novels and comic books—that caught my attention more than anything else? On its surface, the house I grew up in was just another modest upper-middle-class home along the edges of the hills in Sherman Oaks, but below that surface was a hugely dysfunctional gray zone. I grasped that dysfunction at a very early age and checked out, realizing I was alone. As a 1970s kid there were no helicopter parents: you navigated the world more or less on your own, an exploration unaided by parental authority. In retrospect my parents, like the parents of the friends I grew up with, seemed incredibly nonchalant about us, not at all like parents today who document their children's every move on Facebook and pose them on Instagram and urge them into safe spaces and demand only positivity while apparently trying to shelter them from *everything*. If you came of age in the 1970s this was most definitely *not* your childhood. The world wasn't about kids yet.

■ ■ ■

I remember long stretches when I might not have even seen my father apart from the occasional weekday breakfast or dinner on Sunday, as from Monday to Friday he would have left for his job at a downtown real-estate firm before my sisters and I were awake and wouldn't return to the house in Sherman Oaks until we had finished dinner and were contemplating homework in front of the TV sets in our separate bedrooms. At five and six and seven years old, we walked to elementary school by ourselves (parents are now arrested for allowing this) and we played physical games about wars and monsters and espionage throughout the neighborhood streets and up into the canyons that bisected the hills of Sherman Oaks and Studio City and Encino. We would walk home from school alone, grab something to eat in an empty kitchen and then bike a few streets over to someone else's house where it also seemed only kids were living. If we happened to glimpse or actually say hi to somebody's mom, any conversation would be brief and we were always eager to move on, to be on our own again, to find out about the world by ourselves, away from our practically nonexistent parents.

We always seemed to be active, in motion, whether in playgrounds and parks, or splashing in a friend's pool or on the beach wading into the Pacific, or just hanging out at the pinball and video arcade in Westwood Village while Blue Oyster Cult and ELO played as a distant soundtrack over everything. Television consisted of only a few dozen shows that aired nightly on three networks between eight and eleven, and from seven until noon on Saturday mornings—and that was it. Compared to today's choices ours were remarkably sparse, so most of the time we were on suburban streets and in arcades and malls and the beach and at Saturday double and triple matinees on our own, acting out grown-up scenarios by ourselves, feeling our way toward the sexual maturity of adolescence. On a rare weekday afternoon I might stay inside and lounge on the green shag carpet in the living room, or on the waterbed we had, briefly, in the house on Valley Vista, if I was caught up in a comic book or novel I couldn't tear myself away from. At that age I could read a novel in a day, concentrating on nothing else; this was how I absorbed everything from *Harriet the Spy* to the Little House books. But usually I read after dark, deep into the middle of the night, and this was how I first experienced *Carrie*, the novels of James Herbert and the Warren comics I'd become obsessed with during those years—*Eerie*, *Creepy*, *Vampirella*. As a child left to his own devices, all of these horror novels—like the movies I also consumed—confirmed something for me.

I was a child of the '70s who read Thomas Tryon's popular horror novel *The Other* when I was seven years old, balancing the hardcover my mother had checked out of the Sherman Oaks public library on my lap while I waited for another swimming lesson on Ventura Boulevard. The pitchfork death of one of the boys at the end of the first part of that novel stunned me—became *infamous* for me—because it was the only detailed murder I had come across in print, and it has haunted me ever since. I wanted to know on a technical level how the author had pulled this scene off, so I read it over and over again, gazing at the paragraphs, enrapt, figuring out how the author linked the words up to give this scene its charge. The books I read and the movies I watched insisted that the world was a random and cruel place, that danger and death were everywhere, that adults could help you only so much, that there was *another* world—a secret one beneath the fantasy and fake safety of everyday life. Horror movies and horror fiction helped me grasp all of this at an early age. By the time I read Stephen King's *Night Shift*, his first collection of stories in 1978—having already read *Carrie*, *Salem's Lot* and *The Shining* numerous times—few illusions about the supposed neutral innocence of my childhood, or anybody else's, remained.

■ ■ ■

Our parents were lenient about entertainment. R-rated movies were most often okay, and rarely were restrictions placed on what we read or listened to. I remember seeing *National Lampoon's Animal House* with my father at a Saturday matinee in the summer of 1978 at the Avco Theater in Westwood, when I was fourteen and where he and I laughed pretty much nonstop. My father had no problems with the nudity, the sex with a minor, the racy humor (including the dildo Otter holds up), the hand jobs and the topless pillow fights, or with the overall anti-establishment vibe of the picture, which he seemed to enjoy immensely even though he was clearly very much a member of the establishment. (Part of his pleasure had to do with the fact he'd gone to college in the early 1960s as well, the same time as these characters.) I remember my mother clandestinely taking me to a theater in Studio City for a weeknight showing of *Saturday Night Fever* in January 1978 when I was thirteen, because she had a crush on Travolta and we'd been playing the soundtrack for almost two months now in her car after she picked us up from school and drove us to haircuts and piano lessons. (Yes, this was a white, upper-middle-class childhood at the height of Empire.) The movie was a grown-up hard-R thrill and the men in Tony Manero's posse were so powerfully masculine to me they became a big part of my fantasy life until about a year afterward, when Richard Gere pointed me in another direction.

This was a time when parents decided what movies to see and the kids just went. In 1975 I saw Hal Ashby's *Shampoo* on Easter night in Palm Springs with my aunt and two cousins also my age, and my parents who didn't mind that we saw it but were mortified that we turned out to be the only children in the packed theater at the eight p.m. show. As boomers, they thought it made them look bad. *Shampoo* was risqué in ways that my parents weren't expecting—maybe they'd anticipated something frothier, something lighter—and I sat alone in one of the few empty rows up front, away from the rest of the packed theater, blushing deeply. ("I want to suck his *cock*," Julie Christie said drunkenly, gesturing to Warren Beatty at a dinner at the Bistro in Beverly Hills before slipping under the table to blow him.) My pleasure was intensified by how sure I was that my father would have a fit after the movie was over—again, not because of the content, but because bringing his child to this film in front of hundreds of other people had embarrassed him. And he *did* have that fit, even though he pretended not to recognize the three kids trailing after him and my mother and my aunt, as together the adults speed-walked to the car in the theater's parking lot off of North Palm Canyon Drive.

This laissez-faire attitude about content wouldn't be acceptable for most parents today, but it wasn't unusual to be eleven or twelve in the summer of 1976 and to sit through multiple viewings of *The Omen* in a massive theater on a giant screen (brought in by various friends' older siblings because of the R rating and delighted by the slo-mo beheading of David Warner) or to listen to the original cast recording of *A Chorus Line* on 8-track at the same age while being driven somewhere. My sisters and I giggled at "Dance: Ten; Looks: Three" ("*Tits and ass / bought myself a fancy pair / tightened up the derriere*") while our parents sat in the front of the car—my father at the wheel, my mom in the passenger seat—both distracted and nonplussed. We flipped through the Jacqueline Susann and Harold Robbins hardbacks in my grandmother's bookshelf and watched *The Exorcist* on the Z Channel (the country's first pay-cable network that premiered in LA in the mid-'70s) after our parents sternly told us *not* to watch it, but of course we did anyway and got properly freaked out. We saw skits about people doing cocaine on *Saturday Night Live*, and we were drawn to the allure of disco culture and unironic horror movies. We consumed all of this and none of it ever triggered us—we were never wounded because the darkness and the bad mood of the era was everywhere, and when pessimism was the national language, a badge of hipness and cool. Everything was a scam and everybody was corrupt and we were all being raised on a diet of grit. One could argue that this fucked us all up, or maybe, from another angle, it made us stronger. Looking back almost forty years later, it probably made each of us less of a wuss. Yes, we were sixth and seventh graders dealing with a society where no parental filters existed. Tube8.com was not within our reach, fisting videos were not available on our phones, nor were *Fifty Shades of Grey* or gangster rap or violent video games, and terrorism hadn't yet reached our shores, but we were children wandering through a world made almost solely for adults. No one cared what we watched or didn't, how we felt or what we wanted, and we hadn't yet become enthralled by the cult of victimization. It was, by comparison to what's now acceptable when children are coddled into helplessness, an age of innocence.

■ ■ ■

During those years, I spent an inordinate amount of time staring at a movie screen in the darkness of a theater, and so much of it was filled with blood-soaked and realistic and intimate death. Compare and contrast to the bloodless massacres of Marvel films today—what was then PG would probably now be restricted. In one year alone in the mid-'70s I remember witnessing the following: Jill Clayburgh was stabbed to death by George Segal in *The Terminal Man*, a Michael Crichton adaptation that gripped me for a few viewings but now seems unwatchable; Yul Brynner hunted down Richard Benjamin and James Brolin in *Westworld*, the shootings filled with the bright red splatter that flowed across screens in buckets through the middle of the decade; the blood pouring from Donald Sutherland's chopped-open throat at the end of *Don't Look Now* was the same awful color. There was Pamela Franklin being sexually taunted and then killed by the spirits of *The Legend of Hell House*. There was Vincent Price as the deranged actor Edward Lionheart murdering his critics in *Theatre of Blood*, which was one of the more vicious and imaginatively bloody movies I'd ever seen up to that moment. I was nine when my father took me and a friend to an early matinee at the grand art-deco Village Theater in Westwood, a showing that was fairly empty because it was only late morning, and we survived the ordeal, my friend and I delighted by the gory and hideous Shakespearean deaths (including the decapitation of two poodles their owner is forced to consume until he chokes to death). For my father, the movie played as a comedy, which it was, if not for a third grader. He was thirty-two then and not a horror fan, and I think the only reason he decided to chaperone us that April morning was because he had a crush on Diana Rigg, who it turned out was playing Vincent Price's daughter.

I distinctly remember a December afternoon in 1974 when school was out for the holidays and I walked to a theater near our house in Sherman Oaks, the La Reina on Ventura Boulevard, where I watched a matinee of Brian De Palma's *Phantom of the Paradise* and promptly had my young mind blown. At the age of ten I became obsessed by this movie much like I suppose today's pre-millennial generation admires another musical, *Frozen*—but *Phantom of the Paradise* was a flop that no one I knew ever saw, and I would not find any fans of the movie until going to college. (I'd seen it at ten because Pauline Kael, whom I read religiously, had given it a rave in *The New Yorker.*) In this day and in this age, and with many of my friends being parents, I'm somewhat amazed that I (and *my mother*) felt no trepidation about me walking the streets by myself, going to a theater by myself, buying some candy by myself and choosing my seat in some vast and empty auditorium, unaccompanied by any adult, and then proceeding to watch a pretty bloody and sexy movie. Instead, I was thrilled that I was allowed access to this and felt remarkably grown-up, because I didn't need to have a parent holding my hand and horror films were aiding these attempts at independence. If I could survive *Children Shouldn't Play with Dead Things* in a Northridge multiplex with my friend Robert Scarf, or deal with Dirk Benedict's hideous transformation from hot-looking college student to mutated king cobra in *Sssssss* alone in a theater in North Hollywood, or deal with any of the five stories that made up *Tales from the Crypt*, then I felt myself becoming stronger, rising toward something. I was confronting the adult world on my own, by myself, and wrestling with it. There were no adults to answer to, no cell phone they could track me with, I was just alone for three hours on a December afternoon, watching a sophisticated rock-horror musical with some bloody and outrageously satiric scenes and a great set of songs by Paul Williams, and yes, I was ten when this happened. I walked by myself to a Brian De Palma movie and loved it and felt like I was, in the midst of it all, growing up.

■ ■ ■

Not winning but disappointment, disillusionment and pain made joy, happiness, awareness and success both tangible and noticeably more intense, I realized at an early age. We didn't get ribbons for doing a good job and we weren't awarded for just showing up: there were actual winners and losers. School shootings didn't yet exist—at least they weren't epidemic—but we were physically bullied, generally by older kids and usually without parental commiseration or even comment. And we definitely weren't told how special we were at every opportunity. (Yet I can't remember hearing about a single peer's suicide during my childhood and adolescence—either nationally or within the LA private-school system.) It was the out-of-control defiance of horror movies that made this seem like how the world actually works: you win some, you lose some, this is life, this is all preparing me for something, this is normal. These movies reflected the overall disappointment of adulthood and life itself—disappointments I had already witnessed in my parents' failing marriage, my father's alcoholism and my own youthful unhappiness and alienation, which I dealt with and kept processing on my own. The horror movies made in the '70s didn't have rules and often lacked the reassuring backstory that explained the evil away or turned it into a postmodern meta-joke. Why did the killer stalk the sorority girls in *Black Christmas*? Why was Regan possessed in *The Exorcist*? Why was the shark cruising around Amity? Where did Carrie White's powers come from? There were no answers, just as there were no concrete connect-the-dot justifications of daily life's randomness: shit happens, deal with it, stop whining, take your medicine, grow the fuck up. If I often wished the world were a different place, I also knew—and horror movies helped reinforce this—that it *never* would be, a realization that in turn led me to a mode of acceptance. Horror smoothed the transition from the supposed innocence of childhood to the unsurprising disillusionment of adulthood, and it also served to refine my sense of irony.

■ ■ ■

In the summer of 1982, the horror movie I saw right before leaving LA at eighteen to go to college and officially begin my adult life was, tellingly enough, the last one that truly caught me up emotionally, at the time even traumatizing me, disturbing me for years afterward. A group of us went to see John Carpenter's *The Thing* at the Crest Theater in Westwood, having gone the night before to the week's other big opening, Ridley Scott's *Blade Runner* at the Bruin Theater, also in Westwood. (Ultimately, we preferred Carpenter's movie.) *The Thing* takes place in the Antarctic at an American research station, where a group of scientists comes across an alien life form that assimilates and then imitates other organisms. *The Thing* went further than just about any horror movie I'd seen, exploding the body-horror conventions that seemingly had begun with early David Cronenberg and then reached the mainstream with Ridley Scott's *Alien*. And while *Alien* is a smoother, more luxurious nightmare—as well as a truly frightening movie—it ends reassuringly, with the monster dead and Ripley and the cat she saved returning safely to earth. *The Thing* offered no such comfort. Aside from the chest-bursting scene, there's actually very little gore in *Alien*, and what's left is played out in discrete, almost subliminal shock cuts. (Think of how the deaths of Harry Dean Stanton and Yaphet Kotto are shown in tight close-ups.) *The Thing* reverses this aesthetic and doesn't shy away from horror by often relying on extended medium shots and masters where the gruesome assimilations occur, and this presentation so unnerved me—was so bloody, grotesque and absurdist—that I felt I'd finally come to the end of this road. Horror movies just weren't going to affect me in that primitive way anymore. I didn't know it then, that night in the summer of 1982—this realization actually occurred a few months later—but I had become an adult, and I didn't need horror movies the way I once had.

When I came back to Los Angeles that Thanksgiving for a few days, after the shock and delight of being an autonomous freshman at a college far away in the hills of southwestern Vermont for three months, I saw *Creepshow*, a George Romero and Stephen King collaboration, at the same theater where I'd seen *Theatre of Blood* with my friend and my father almost a decade earlier, and I just shrugged at it. I had already completed my education.

acting

woman, a divorcée who lives in Malibu, played by Nina Van Pallandt, and the other is a big, bad black man played by Bill Duke, who lives on the West Side in a high-rise festooned with Warhol prints. We're not sure if the woman knows about the other pimp—maybe this matters at first, maybe it doesn't, but what *does* matter is that Julian is a happy, superficial capitalist with very little backstory. He just exists, floating through this world, an actor. He tells someone at one point that he was born in Torino, but we don't know if this is true because in the previous scene he lied to a client about being a pool boy at the Beverly Hills Hotel in his youth. The engine of the plot kicks in when Julian is framed for a murder, and *American Gigolo* becomes a crime thriller. Narratively, it's somewhat standard, and its resolution is clean and simple. But none of that matters because the movie's design is so seductive and stunning.

American Gigolo was Paul Schrader's third movie as a young director and everything he learned on his first two pays off here: the gliding camera movements, the gorgeous sets, the dramatic lighting—all aiding in the creation of his acid vision of Los Angeles as a brightly colored wasteland. This is a sunlit neo-noir, ominous and beautiful, and it was of its moment: there was something late-'70s New Wave about it, minimal and chic, lush and corrosive, and there was something gay about it as well, which then seemed everywhere in the culture. Mainstream audiences had never seen a man photographed—objectified—the way Richard Gere was. The camera ogled his beauty, roamed over his skin, devoured his adolescent petulance, was hypnotized by his flesh, and Gere was the first leading man in a big studio movie to go full frontal. Originally, John Travolta was going to star in *American Gigolo* but walked away just weeks before production, and an

In February 1980, when I was fifteen, I saw Paul Schrader's *American Gigolo* at the National Theatre in Westwood and had no idea the movie was influenced by Robert Bresson, the French minimalist filmmaker, or that the ending—a fake alibi one character offers another—was lifted from Bresson's film *Pickpocket*. (In 2012 when I was writing the screenplay for Schrader's *The Canyons*, my penultimate scene involved a version of that alibi between Lindsay Lohan and James Deen, an updated riff on *Pickpocket*'s final moment, but *Gigolo* was my model there, not Bresson.) Looking back, the impact *American Gigolo* had on me is impossible to tally, and it's not as if this is a great film—it's not, and even its director agrees—but in the way it changed how we look at and objectify men, and altered how I thought about and experienced LA, its influence is vast and undeniable. The film is set in 1979 Los Angeles, whose denizens dine at Ma Maison and Perino's and Scandia and Le Dome—and Julian Kay, the title character, is living in a chic Westwood apartment, adorned in Armani, driving the empty streets in a Mercedes convertible and making his living as a male prostitute for wealthy older women while haunting the Polo Lounge in the Beverly Hills Hotel, and he is extraordinarily beautiful—the movie captures Richard Gere at the height of his beauty, when he was thirty but looks younger. Julian has two pimps who supply him with work: one is a blond audience might have rooted for Travolta's earnestness more than Gere's blankness; Travolta might have humanized the movie—instinctively brought humor to it—and would have given it a realism. But with Gere at its center, the movie is a chilly and remote experience, and at this point in his career humor eludes him. There's a sadness to Gere, yet this doesn't erase the notion that Julian Kay is less a character than an idea, an abstraction, an actor, and he's certainly not likable.

And yet Gere's blankness and the movie's austerity collided, and audiences went with it in the spring of 1980 and made him a star. The model Lauren Hutton plays Michelle, the unhappy wife of a California senator, and she's quite stunning as well, but the movie loves its leading man—the tension comes from Gere's beauty and narcissism. Women had always been photographed like this, but men hadn't—it was new, it was gay, it ended up influencing everything from the popularity of GQ magazine to how Calvin Klein began advertising men. In retrospect, it's amazing that *American Gigolo* was a hit: the film is deliberately paced, sometimes glacially so, and flirts with pretension more often than it doesn't, so it's hard to believe this art object with very few commercial concessions (except, of course, that delirious come-on of a title) was in fact a big Paramount picture produced by Jerry Bruckheimer.

■ ■ ■

In 1980 I was beginning the *Less Than Zero* project which would culminate in 1985 with my first novel's publication, and though I took many of my cues from Joan Didion and LA noir, along with bands like the Doors and X and the Eagles, *American Gigolo* was another key template so much so that I named the male teenage prostitute Julian as well. What I responded to at fifteen was the moral ambiguity of not only the subject matter, and of Julian Kay himself, but also the filmmaking: I couldn't make up my mind about what the movie was selling me—and I liked that. Blondie's electrifying "Call Me" burst over the opening credits like an anthem, though the movie was basically dark and pessimistic with Richard Gere's beauty offered as something to crave, while at the same time something deeply ambiguous. That fall, Robert Redford's *Ordinary People* spoke most passionately to my sixteen-year-old self, with Timothy Hutton as the movie character I most identified with, but now I can barely watch it. For all its flaws, I can watch *American Gigolo* endlessly. It came out when films could have a kind of far-ranging cultural influence, just as novels could, and both movies and novels now look like art forms of the twentieth century, not the twenty-first. Movies no longer work for us as an exploration of unseen, faraway cultures, unless they're otherworldly and fantastical. We're no longer impelled to go to a theater simply to see Richard Gere standing naked in his Westwood apartment, maneuvering through the gay men dancing at the Probe on North Highland Avenue or just hanging out on sunlit Rodeo Drive—to live as voyeurs of the wealthy world of Beverly Hills in which *American Gigolo* takes place. All this is over: reality TV and Instagram have replaced it.

■ ■ ■

Julian Kay is an actor—and Gere's performance is a performance of a performance. *American Gigolo*'s narrative trajectory is that of a performer who needs to become real and get off the stage in order to save himself. Of course, this is the standard loss-of-innocence arc that's found in most American movies, except here it's more interesting and literally superficial than usual, as is the actor's performance. I'd become aware of Gere a few years before while watching the Z Channel in my Sherman Oaks bedroom and saw him costarring in the overwrought 1977 adaptation of Judith Rossner's 1975 best seller, *Looking for Mr. Goodbar.* (I read my mom's copy of the novel when I was eleven.) About forty-five minutes into the movie he appears as Tony, one of Diane Keaton's pickups. She first notices him at a singles bar because he's about to steal a wallet out of someone's purse—but why wouldn't she notice him anyway? He's beautiful. In the following scene Gere brings Keaton to orgasm in her apartment while Donna Summer sings "Could It Be Magic" and then performs a balletic mock-rumble kung-fu dance in his jockstrap while brandishing a glow-in-the-dark switchblade. All of this was electrifyingly sexy to my eighth-grade sensibility (it's ludicrous now) and in an erotic trance I began following Gere's career through 1978 (*Days of Heaven, Bloodbrothers*) and into 1979 (*Yanks*), developing a full-blown teenage fixation. It could have been anyone, I guess, but the timing of my adolescence and of these movies made for another collision.

In this phase of his career Gere represented a gritty 1970s male sensuality and seemed perfectly cast in the downbeat, nihilistic world of *Looking for Mr. Goodbar,* whose story was yet another one of that decade's archetypical narratives. Schoolteacher Theresa Dunn's murder at the hands of a random sex partner in the mid-'70s urban wasteland of Manhattan was sexually arousing and had a tabloid excitement for me at fourteen, but it also alternately horrified and bored and depressed me. Diane Keaton experiences her ultimate orgasm as she's being stabbed to death on another one-night stand (by Tom Berenger, another fixation of mine from that moment) beneath the flickering dead end of a strobe light, gasping and covered with blood—punishment achieved and morality play completed. And yet I watched the film over and over again during the weeks it played on the Z Channel, for glimpses of Gere.

In 1979, the only movie he appeared in was *Yanks*, John Schlesinger's World War II ensemble about GIs stationed in northern England in 1943. It was the first time Gere had starred in a movie made by a gay director, and the difference between this and his two previous movies (one directed by Terrence Malick, the other by Robert Mulligan) was noticeable to me even at fifteen. Everything changed because the camera now approached Gere as a *star*, accentuating the sad almond eyes, the sensuous full-lipped mouth, the glamorous hollowed-out cheeks, the smooth ex-gymnast's body that we glimpse naked in a barracks shower in one of the very first scenes—the blocking somewhat obscures explicit nudity, but we get the idea—and his prominent nose seemed less schnozzy: someone in lust was photographing him. Watching *Yanks* for the first time that fall when I was fifteen, I hadn't before seen a more beautiful man in any movie, but he also seemed blank and lost, which probably added to his beauty. Gere's flaw in period films like *Days of Heaven* and *Yanks* was that he seemed too contemporary, too modern, to truly fit into these worlds, and because of this he was mannered. He comes off in *Yanks* as amateurish, with a flat and uninflected voice, and he doesn't look or sound or move the way we'd imagine a wisecracking short-order cook from Arizona would—he seems instead as if he should be preening on the catwalk in late-'70s Milan, twitchy from drugs and open to anything sexually, or else lounging around Studio 54 and the Fiorucci boutique in Beverly Hills. Gere emanates a sense of entitlement that seems faintly bizarre, yet he holds the screen even as it is almost always apparent that he's acting, and overly self-aware, never really disappearing into the role. There remains a genuine tension in this.

Yanks is a glazed and somewhat embalmed piece of traditional studio moviemaking, and all the Americans are miscast: Chick Vennera as Gere's best friend is encouraged to overdo everything, and who in their right mind considered William Devane a romantic leading man, paired with the luminous Vanessa Redgrave no less? It was a major bomb, but Gere had already shot *American Gigolo* by the time *Yanks* flopped. This was the second movie in which he'd replaced Travolta (the first was *Days of Heaven*), and though Paramount wanted Christopher Reeve for Julian Kay after Travolta split, Paul Schrader held out for Gere, finally convincing the head of the studio, Barry Diller, to cast him. (Julie Christie dropped out after Travolta left, and Meryl Streep later turned down the role of Michelle because she found the script distasteful.) In the opening half of *American Gigolo*, it's obvious that Julian Kay will be anyone you want, depending on how much you pay him. One of the first times we see him he's hanging upside down in his apartment, wearing gravity boots while rehearsing lines in Swedish for an upcoming eight-thousand-dollar trick, and later he runs the same lines with that senator's wife, Michelle. Sometimes he's a chauffeur for a wealthy widow from Charlottesville, and then he turns into a swishy German decorator in order to protect a client when they're visiting Sotheby's—arguably one of Gere's more embarrassing moments on screen. In the movie's most iconic scene Julian gets dressed for a night out, wiping cocaine off a small mirror, laying out beautiful Armani suits on his bed, choosing a costume, inspecting the drawers of luxurious shirts and shimmering ties while Smokey Robinson sings "The Love I Saw in You Was Just a Mirage." Near the end of the movie, Julian desperately tells the pimp who set him up for the Rheiman murder in Palm Springs that he'll play other roles (gay, kink) in order to escape this frame-up, and you realize that *American Gigolo* could be considered a horror movie about an actor losing his audience. Julian thinks he's free but he's constantly told what to do—everything's really just an audition to get paid.

■ ■ ■

I've been involved with actors since I was a child, in close proximity from elementary school and high school into adulthood, both professionally and a few times romantically. Even with the crazy passive-aggressive positivity actors need simply to maintain their balance and to feed their hunger to seduce and control you, I've always found them endearing and likable. This neurosis is ultimately forgivable since this is what actors are *supposed* to do—to make you like them. Their job simply demands: *I want to make you want me.* And because of this, at least for the majority of actors whom I've hung out with, acting is a hard life, filled with a low-level fear and emotional peril due to what might happen if you *don't* like them. What if you don't respond to what they're selling?

It's pretty basic: what happens if the actor *just isn't liked*? This is not a job that's forced on anyone; it's simply *chosen* by people who want to express themselves (regardless of where their neuroses come from) and also hope to make a living from doing so. But most actors never succeed, and the struggle and rejection inherent in their trade makes just about any other profession seem sane and straightforward. The reasons an actor is *wanted* and hired are so random—often luck based, having nothing to do with merit and capability—that watching this game from the sidelines, as a nonactor, can be upsetting enough to make your mind reel. (This is why I find casting sessions almost unbearable—even before hearing someone read from the script, from the moment they walk into the room I can tell instantly whether he or she is right for the role, or not.) Imagine, then, what this feels like for *them*. Actors are so integral to film and theater and TV that the best of them unearth truths that are stunningly revealing, and they can also be a joy to watch because of their physicality as well as their talent. Who has a problem looking at amazingly pretty people for the duration of even a mediocre movie? Actors *depend* on their likability, and their attractiveness, because they *want* people to watch them, to be drawn to them, to desire them. Because of this, actors are, by their very nature, liars.

For this reason, they end up playing a part for us in their lives, too. And they can't help it: they spend their days disappearing into personas. They want to please, they want to do a good job, they have a need—and because of this actors can be as simple and amiable and guileless as the friendliest golden retriever. Or they can be paranoid and emotionally needy narcissists, always worrying about what anyone and everyone wants from them. Is it just a job? Is it only a performance? Do they want sexual gratification? What role should I play to get this part? How high do I turn the sexual wattage up for the casting director, this producer, that executive? *God, I hope they like me.* Actors dread criticism and are more wounded by it because, unlike most of us, they live in front of an audience, and criticism means the public might not like them anymore. Criticism means the next job, that next flirtation, maybe the big career-changing payday might not happen. For the actor, criticism is tied far more intimately to survival than it is for any of the rest of us. Or at least it hasn't been, until lately.

■ ■ ■

A long time ago in the faraway era of Empire, actors could protect their carefully designed and enigmatic selves more easily and completely than is possible now, when we all live in the digital land of social media where our phones candidly capture moments that used to be private and our unbidden thoughts can be typed up in a line or two on Twitter. Some actors have become more hidden, less likely to go public with their opinions, likes and dislikes—because who knows where that next job's coming from? Others have become more vocal, stridently voicing their righteousness, but signaling one's social-justice virtue isn't necessarily the same as being honest—it can also be a pose. Who might these actors offend if they behaved like regular people, angry and riddled with contradictions? But being an actor involves turning into a blank, hollowing yourself out so you can replace whatever was there with the character you're playing next. What does it mean to *be real* as an actor? What does transparency mean if you're essentially a vessel waiting to be filled again and again and again? Part of the actor's immediate charm stems from an upbeat attitude they keep selling, one that masks their true selves. If you get to know an actor intimately you might or might not have access to that true self in private, but rarely will you see it in public, where the actor always continues to play a part. But most of us now lead lives on social media that are more performance based than we ever could have imagined even a decade ago, and thanks to this burgeoning cult of likability, in a sense, we've *all* become actors. We've had to rethink the means with which to express our feelings and thoughts and ideas and opinions in the void created by a corporate culture that is forever trying to silence us by sucking up everything human and contradictory and *real* with its assigned rule book on how to behave. We seem to have entered precariously into a kind of totalitarianism that actually abhors free speech and punishes people for revealing their true selves. In other words: the actor's dream.

■ ■ ■

In May 1985 *Less Than Zero* was published, and even though it didn't become a national best seller until the fall, it was talked about in certain publishing circles and it wasn't long before magazines started asking me—a junior at Bennington College—to write articles for them. One of the first was *Vanity Fair*, whose editor in chief summoned me to New York that July when I was attending the Bennington writers summer workshop in Vermont. I took the train down to Manhattan and arrived, somewhat nervously, at the bar at the Algonquin to meet the woman who had revived *Vanity Fair* into what was becoming once again the buzziest magazine around. I sat across from her and was immediately uncomfortable: Tina Brown was soft-spoken, petite, with a no-nonsense air of British formality, and she could stare you down with a laser-light intensity. I found her stillness intimidating, so as a hungover, shaggy twenty-one-year-old I ordered a midday vodka and grapefruit juice to settle my nerves. She wanted to know what I might like to write about, and I shrugged because I really didn't have a clue. I wasn't even sure I wanted to write a piece for the magazine, and I finally told her so. But she persisted, sometimes silently. Tina's silences were always weighted with meanings I couldn't decipher, and she didn't seem to care how long they lasted. I remember an especially lengthy one that went on for minutes when we had lunch in the late '90s at the Royalton, when she wanted me to write a profile of the then-recluse Axl Rose for *The New Yorker*, where she had become editor in chief. (I demurred.) I was used to all this by then, but at the Algonquin, a decade earlier, I kept shifting uncomfortably. And then she brought up the Brat Pack, who had been newly branded in a recent *New York* magazine piece.

"Is there an actor in the Brat Pack that you might like to profile?" Tina asked. I shrugged. "What about Judd Nelson?" she suggested quietly. *St. Elmo's Fire* had opened a few weeks earlier and I'd seen *The Breakfast Club* that spring. "Yeah, maybe . . ." Now it was my turn to go silent. She looked at something on the table, then back at me. "He's quite annoying, isn't he?" I made a meaningless gesture with my hands. "Yeah, I guess . . ." "I think he's quite annoying," she said again, then asked, "Don't you?" I'd never met Judd Nelson and told her so. "He seems a bit obnoxious," she insisted. "That might be a very interesting match—you profiling Judd." Something seemed to be swirling around the bar in the Algonquin that summer afternoon: she was beginning to get to me and I was seeing things her way, and soon I began to nod. "Yeah, yeah, he does seem pretty annoying," I said. "You're right." Tina then asked when I'd next be in LA and said she was hoping to get the piece ready for *Vanity Fair*'s Los Angeles issue, which would be out in October. I told her I'd get back to LA in August when the workshop was over, and she said she'd handle all the necessary arrangements. I left the hotel in a kind of daze, worried that I'd mindlessly accepted an assignment that in the end would somehow displease her. She seemed so exacting and the magazine itself so impossibly glamorous to my college-kid sensibility, and did I really want to do a hit piece on an actor? But I found out from my agent later that afternoon what I would get paid and it staggered me—"A fuck of a lot of money," as she put it—and by comparison to the digital age when everyone basically writes for free, it seems even more staggering in retrospect. And so the plan was set in motion: I would meet the actor Judd Nelson, find him appalling, and write about how awful hanging out with him had been.

I realized later—I didn't make the connection in the bar—that Tina had of course read *New York*'s Brat Pack article. It was the most talked-about piece of celebrity journalism in years. The magazine had sent David Blum to Los Angeles to profile Emilio Estevez, arguably the most famous of the actors in Joel Schumacher's recently released *St. Elmo's Fire*, and what had been pitched as a typical puff piece quickly warped into a scathing portrayal that soon became scandalous. Estevez's mistake was inviting the journalist to trail him around LA, allowing him to observe what young stars do with their nights off. It's all quite harmless: nobody's snorting blow or banging hookers, it's just Emilio using his new status to get into nightclubs and comped at movie theaters, but the authorial tone makes everyone in the piece, no matter what they're doing or saying, *seem* entitled and annoying. Its chief weakness—and the reason I'm mystified why it has carried such pop-cultural weight for more than three decades—is that the only people in it besides Estevez are the barely present Rob Lowe and Judd Nelson, for whom Blum reserves the bulk of his ire. Timothy Hutton makes a brief appearance, but he was never part of the Brat Pack; he'd become a star five years earlier and had already won an Oscar. But Blum lumps everyone from that period together, including Tom Cruise, Matt Dillon, Matthew Broderick, Matthew Modine and Nic Cage. And so begins a curious study in journalistic pathology: a youngish male reporter (Blum was probably thirty at the time) seems to seethe over the beauty and good fortune of these up-and-coming young actors, so he twists their youthful nights out—drinking Coronas at the Hard Rock, reveling in the attention from starstruck girls—into something almost sinister.

■ ■ ■

Because of the roles Nelson had played in *The Breakfast Club* and *St. Elmo's Fire*, as well as in a little-seen movie I'd caught earlier that year called *Fandango*, and because by now I'd read the *New York* Brat Pack piece, I wasn't sure whom I was going to meet, and because I had been influenced and flattered by Tina

Brown, I expected to dislike him. But Judd was nothing like the snarling John Bender in *The Breakfast Club* or the entitled yuppie Alec from *St. Elmo's Fire*, or anything I had inferred from another magazine's previous snarky profile—he was smart, funny, direct, likable. And because we were getting along so well I decided, while we were sitting in Carney's on Sunset Boulevard on the afternoon we met in August of 1985, to confide what my editor had in mind for the piece, and what she was probably expecting me to turn in. Judd contemplated this, and we went back and forth on how to approach this problem, and the *unfairness* of it all, whether real or imagined, and then came up with an alternative. Instead of a Judd Nelson profile we offered *Vanity Fair* a piece about where young Hollywood *really* hangs out—not Spago and the Roxy, but the secret places where the hip and connected actually *go*. We envisioned "Looking for Cool in LA." When I pitched the piece to the magazine they loved it, even bringing handsome young Bradford Branson on board to shoot the places Judd and I had decided to extol as LA's coolest. What I didn't let anyone at *Vanity Fair* know was that the places Judd and I would sanctify were actually some of the most retrograde, least fashionable venues in greater Los Angeles—places that real young Hollywood sophisticates not only would shun, but probably hadn't even heard of.

Where did LA's youngest and hippest prefer to eat? At Philippe: the original home of the French-dip sandwich, a simple cafeteria on Alameda and Ord. For a cultural excursion: the Museum of Neon Art. The coolest place for a drink would be the bar at the downtown Hilton on a seedy stretch of Wilshire Boulevard. And then there was the fictional Bud Club—a legendary floating emporium that could magically pop up anywhere from Glendale to dark and deserted Venice, so elusive that it allegedly drove the young and hip insane. Everywhere from the retro coffee shop Ben Frank's to a Chinese fortune-teller hidden in the outskirts of Pasadena became the fake go-to for LA's juvenile elite—and Judd and I sold them all, posing at each in black suits and skinny ties and Ray-Bans for photographs Brandon shot in beautiful shimmering black and white. To make sure nobody at the magazine would get suspicious we threw in a few legitimately trendy places: Power Tools, the Ritz Café, Chianti Cucina, Dirt Box. Ultimately, the two of us felt that we had both dodged a bullet—me having something stranger and less orthodox than a hack profile could offer, and Judd going unscathed by an encounter with a potentially dubious journalist. The piece ran in the November 1985 issue, our names heralded on the cover and superimposed over Sylvester Stallone posing with Brigitte Nielsen. As a senior at Bennington College I remember opening that issue on a bus heading from campus into town and feeling both delighted and frightened by what Judd and I had pulled off, and it wasn't long before I heard that *Vanity Fair* had found out what we'd perpetrated, and understandably I was never asked to write anything else during Tina Brown's reign. Ironically, a few of the places we prematurely proclaimed cool ultimately became so for a little while, because of the piece, and it seems a reminder now of the power of *Vanity Fair*, of youth, and of the 1980s.

■ ■ ■

Simon & Schuster announced a first printing of five thousand copies of *Less Than Zero*, expecting to sell maybe half that amount. In the spring of 1985, I honestly didn't care how many copies it sold—I was just amazed the book even got published, that something I'd been working on for five years was going to be an actual hardcover sold in real bookstores. In the long ago Empire of America it took much longer than it does now not only for a novel to catch on with what was then a more substantial reading public, but also for actual books to make it into actual bookstores, which was where we all went to buy a book. We might spend an hour there, browsing the aisles, a favorite pastime of mine that's now just about impossible to replicate, so many of us having been lured away from brick-and-mortar shops by the ease of Amazon, and their promise to deliver a copy to our mailbox the day the book is officially published. This wasn't the case in May 1985, when a first novel by a writer nobody had ever heard of left a warehouse and was slowly made available through the rest of the country over the summer and even into the fall. And it wasn't until October that the book appeared on *The New York Times* best-seller list. Though hardly a blockbuster, it sold well for a first novel and it was a genuine word-of-mouth success, since Simon & Schuster had initially budgeted no money to promote and advertise it.

But the media, almost immediately, grew curious and began writing about both the book and its author, and—for whatever reason—*Less Than Zero* soon started to connect with a large and youthful audience that saw itself mirrored in its attitude and sensibility. The novel seemed to confirm something for many people, as if it were a news bulletin from the front lines—this is what kids are like today!—rather than a highly personal novel that I'd been working on, in one form or another, since I was sixteen. But when I finally finished it, at twenty, the book ultimately *did* feel like a reflection of where we were in the moment and not just an autobiographical story—the narrator was always both me and not me. Or perhaps the real appeal was the spell it cast for readers thousands of miles away from Southern California: What would it *really* be like to live in this Beverly Hills fantasy that they felt was so cool? This was often, I found out in fan letters, the takeaway for young readers in Indiana, in the UK, in New Delhi.

■ ■ ■

Our tour guide through *Less Than Zero* is handsome and pale Clay—eighteen, passive, druggy, bi. A boy profoundly disconnected from just about everyone: his family; his girlfriend, Blair; and his friends, among them Julian, who turns tricks with older men in order to pay off a drug debt. There's no real plot until the last quarter of the book; the story's told in fragments, a mosaic, and the details keep adding up with, hopefully, a quiet menace. There's no love, and no real friendship: money, teenage sex and easy access to drugs open the door to a kind of gleaming nihilism. "Disappear Here" the book keeps insisting, quoting a billboard on Sunset Boulevard that haunts Clay. Part of the book's appeal to young readers could be that they'd never been presented quite like this in contemporary American fiction before: as sophisticated teenagers who aped the attitudes of their materialistic and narcissistic boomer parents. But *Less Than Zero* doesn't blame the parents. And in fact it's still rare for a young person's novel to feature kids who are just as bad as their parents, if not even worse. Most of those parents are demonized, but the parents in was never going to be a family-friendly enterprise. If Fox wanted to make an honest re-creation of the book they would have to go all the way, because a compromised version was never going to work: it wouldn't be the thing readers had initially responded to, which was the cool numbness of it all.

Fox brought in Jon Avnet, who had successfully produced *Risky Business*, a big hit featuring upper-middle-class teenagers that made Tom Cruise a star, but Avnet considered the Michael Cristofer script "depressing and degrading" and you began to wonder if Avnet had ever read the book, because he now wanted to "transform a very extreme situation into a sentimental story about warmth, caring and tenderness in an atmosphere hostile to those kinds of emotions." Larry Gordon, the president of Fox when the book was purchased, had been replaced by Leonard Goldberg, who, unlike the other players at the studio, was a family man, and he found the material distasteful, but Barry Diller persisted and wanted the movie made. Everyone just needed to get on the same page and figure out how to do it. The screenwriter Harley Peyton was hired to write a new script where Clay's bisexuality and drug use were eliminated in a narrative that no longer presented him as passive and "amoral," and yet executives at the studio *still* worried that it was too edgy a proposition for even eight million dollars, which wasn't a lot of money for a studio film in the 1980s. But they believed, however, that they'd found the right director: Marek Kanievska, a Brit who was hired because he'd dealt with ambivalent sexuality before and had made "unlikable" characters appealing in his film *Another Country*, which featured Rupert Everett in a role loosely based on Guy Burgess, the famous—and gay—spy.

So shooting commenced, but ultimately Fox took the movie

Less Than Zero are rarely on display at all. It's kids left to their own devices who have tripped themselves into this world of too much money, too many drugs and too much entitlement who become their own worst enemies. The novel also reflects a numbness that was pervasive in the culture, particularly in Los Angeles, when I started writing it in 1980—a numbness that was thrilling and yet also contrary to reflexive understanding, to genuine feeling as well.

■ ■ ■

The movie rights were optioned before publication by an independent producer named Marvin Worth (*Lenny*, *The Rose*), who had a deal with 20th Century Fox, the studio that would be financing the movie. The purchase on their end was sponsored by Scott Rudin and Larry Mark, who were the vice presidents of production under Barry Diller, who, at that time, was the studio's chairman—and all three of them wanted this movie to happen. The first script was written by the Pulitzer Prize–winning playwright Michael Cristofer, but Fox thought it was too harsh for a "commercial" film and already we'd reached a divide between the novel and the adaptation. Why buy the rights to *Less Than Zero* if you weren't going to accept the *spirit* of the book? Since the novel had quickly become a touchstone for young people, maybe the studio could roll the dice and make some money by adapting faithfully what was already a well-known title. But we were never talking about a sure thing—unlike *The Fault in Our Stars*, *Less Than Zero* hadn't sold eighteen million copies—and this away from Kanievska because, according to people on set, he kept making it edgier and straying too dangerously close in spirit to the source material. The cinematographer Edward Lachman later recalled that the studio hated his incredible Steadicam shot of the (then unknown) Red Hot Chili Peppers performing at a club, because the band was "shirtless and sweaty," and Fox demanded that the shot be removed. Early test-screening audiences between the ages of fifteen and twenty-one revealed that they hated the Robert Downey Jr. character, so new scenes were shot to make his character more "likable" and "repentant"—that was the studio's word: "repentant." The lavish high-school graduation sequence that opens the movie was part of the reshoots, and it now contained a lot of smiling and good vibes along with champagne bottles being popped.

■ ■ ■

Because of all this panic and wrangling, something's off in the finished product: it doesn't work dramatically. In the opening, pre-credit sequence there are already strained plot devices that begin to engulf the movie: expressions of intense emotion from the main characters that aren't in the book, a push for everyone to be likable. Clay and Julian and Blair are now a team, happily graduating from high school on a sunny day and looking forward to the summer and beyond. In flashbacks, Clay recalls these events from his chic dorm room somewhere on the East Coast, and it seems that he and Julian are best friends, and Blair is his main squeeze. Julian has stayed in LA to pursue a career as a record producer-slash-club promoter, and Blair wants to concentrate on her modeling career rather than go to college. (In the book Blair attends the University of Southern California.) In the movie, during Clay's first term away, Julian becomes impossibly addicted to drugs, and he and Blair end up sleeping together. Clay discovers this when he returns to LA at Thanksgiving break for a surprise visit, only to find the two of them in bed in Blair's beautiful downtown loft. And so, a love triangle's set up. A conventional narrative structure has been imposed upon a book where narrative is nonexistent, and this now needs to resolve itself, because the movie—even before the opening credits roll—has set this particular storyline in motion.

Clay is now upstanding: antidrug, resolutely heterosexual and prone to chastising everyone for his or her behavior, the ultimate Jewish mother. The Clay from the book who doesn't care about anything or pretends not to is now the uptight center of the movie. This choice straitjackets a panicked-looking Andrew McCarthy, who had already become a go-to guy for Gen-X stoicism and moral despair, and his presence here is a drag, wholesome and preppy and whitewashed. (My first choice for Clay had been Anthony Michael Hall, which the studio rejected as they did my first choice for director, Walter Hill.) Downey tries hard to make Julian, the novel's unreachable nihilist, lost and lovable, and the book's smart-spoiled tough girl Blair, who knows all this is a total mess and a scam, becomes the super-jittery and helpless Jami Gertz, teary-eyed and earnest and completely miscast. The supposed "heat" between McCarthy and Gertz (which isn't in the book) is especially iffy, even though they are constantly making out and have to simulate sex twice. There's even a scene in which McCarthy has to fake an orgasm when Gertz gives him a hand job in his vintage convertible Corvette spinning wheelies on Rodeo Drive, as a biker gang zooms by. The credit sequence, with neon-red block lettering and the Bangles cover of "Hazy Shade of Winter" blasting over it, still feels somewhat iconic, but watching Clay smile in recognition at familiar landmarks (the Hard Rock Cafe, and, oddly enough, the Beverly Hills boutique Giorgio) once he's back in LA for Christmas break, craning his neck out of the cab to get a better look, is flatly bizarre, because he'd been here just three weeks earlier yet seems to have little trepidation about returning to a city where he grew up and is now problematic in troublesome new ways since he discovered his best friend and girlfriend are an item—happily taking in these sights makes no sense. None of this is drawn from the novel, where I don't think there's a single scene when Julian and Blair are even in the same room together.

Edward Lachman ends up being the key creative artist in *Less Than Zero*—the film is gorgeously lit and shot. Visually, the movie's often stunningly beautiful, accentuating massive open spaces that suggest the loneliness of LA, and the sets are spectacular: there's an over-the-top Beverly Hills Christmas party complete with fake snow and hundreds of extras (Brad Pitt is one of them), and fake icebergs dotted with video monitors and giant Christmas trees dusted white, all of which propose that this is ostensibly a movie about cocaine, and its grandeur might remind you that this kind of movie will never be made again on such a lavish scale. As an artifact from that era it's unparalleled: no other youth-culture movie set in LA has such an epic look, certainly compared to *Valley Girl* or *Fast Times at Ridgemont High* (both better movies by the way). And yet it doesn't work because it betrays the source material and takes the punk nihilism that influenced the novel and squeezes it into a big, teen-friendly, mainstream studio movie—about "friendship" with way too much smiling: *tearful* smiling, *sexy* smiling, *happy* and *sad* smiling—which creates an incredibly lopsided experience. The movie's earnestness and yearning to be likable and relatable is what ultimately kills it.

▪ ▪ ▪

A week before the movie's release, and just a few days before I was planning to see it screened at Fox's offices in Manhattan, Marek Kanievska called to say he needed to see me. We hadn't met but I was close friends with a woman who'd had an affair with him during postproduction and told me about the problems Marek was having with the studio, so I had some ideas about the difficulties he'd had. Marek wanted to meet at six o'clock at Nell's, a popular nightclub that I was frequenting then, though I doubted that Nell's was open that early but it turned out to be, sort of. Only Marek and his date were sitting in a booth in the otherwise dark and deserted space, and I realized that the club had been opened for him—a friend of the Brit Pack that owned and operated Nell's—and also that I'd never been there much earlier than midnight. I also realized I hadn't heard anything specific about the movie itself because having graduated from college only a year earlier, I'd just recently moved to New York and was working on a new novel and more interested in other things. I'd only skimmed the Michael Cristofer script but I'd never read the Harley Peyton draft.

When I sat down Marek was slumped over in the booth,

already drunk. My initial smile froze as he started talking: "I'm so so sorry for how the movie turned out. I tried my best, I fought the battles, I lost. I'm so so sorry." And because of this, I was prepared later that week when I watched the movie in a packed screening room where I'd invited friends, people from MTV, the VJs of the moment, several actors I knew. It didn't take very long to tell something was wrong, and for my excitement of seeing my fictional world visualized to quickly fade. As the movie crept to an end, it dawned on me that there hadn't been a single scene or line of dialogue in the movie that was taken from the book. Marek Kanievska didn't direct another film for thirteen years. Oddly enough, that one—*Where the Money Is*, starring Paul Newman—and *American Psycho* opened the same week in 2000, and *American Psycho* beat it at the box office.

■ ■ ■

In an unpublished forward to his 1964 autobiography, Charlie Chaplin wrote, "In this record I shall tell only what I want to tell, for there is a line of demarcation between oneself and the public. There are some things which if divulged to the public, I would have nothing left to hold body and soul together, and my personality would disappear like the waters of the rivers that flow into the sea." I thought about this quote recently, after having Judd Nelson on a podcast I hosted infrequently starting in the fall of 2013 and into the late spring of 2017, because it seemed like the perfect summation of something I'd detected with a number of actors I'd talked with on that PodcastOne show. I hadn't seen

Judd in nearly twenty-five years when I invited him to participate, ostensibly to discuss *The Breakfast Club* on its thirtieth anniversary but actually because I remember him back in those days as intelligent and outspoken and completely realistic about Hollywood; in particular, he'd told hilarious stories about the troubled production of *St. Elmo's Fire.* In real life he was closer to a male version of Molly Ringwald's Claire Standish, and if that sounds prim and unattractive, it wasn't. This was the private Judd I'd spent time with at the height of his brief fame, and when I greeted him, now in his midfifties, at the podcast studio in Beverly Hills, I wasn't surprised that he seemed to have mellowed out. But the private person I had expected to shine on the podcast never really showed up in front of the microphone.

The frazzled and funny Judd still existed, but not necessarily in public. In the studio when I asked how tricky the *St. Elmo's Fire* shoot had really been, he hesitated and answered diplomatically even though it had taken place more than thirty years earlier and everyone's career had by now come and gone, and I realized then that he was putting on a performance—wanting to be liked, wanting to sell himself—and anything that sounded critical or *negative* wasn't going to help his cause. The only criticism he volunteered that hour, in fact, was directed at the journalist who had trashed him in that *New York* magazine piece about the Brat Pack. Yet after the podcast, while we were standing around the parking garage of PodcastOne, Judd started regaling me and my producer with those stories about making *St. Elmo's Fire*. I interrupted him to ask why he hadn't talked about any of this on the show where I had prodded him gently and then less gently but then stopped when it became obvious he simply wasn't willing to go there. When we scheduled his appearance I'd assured Judd this wasn't a shock-jock podcast and we weren't hunting for or addicted to controversy, but afterward he explained that he wasn't in the business of telling tales out of school.

There in the garage, I asked who exactly might be offended: *St. Elmo's Fire*'s somewhat flamboyant director, Joel Schumacher? Or was it *Jo-elle Shoo-ma-Shay*, as I remembered some cast members called him when we were hanging out together in the summer of 1985? Weren't the stories of drugs and Demi Moore already out there—was this *really* a problem? But Judd considered these sorts of truths *negatively*. There were other topics we hadn't hit during that hour though, and he agreed to come back and record some stuff that we could edit into the episode before we posted it. I emailed him later that day inviting him back, offering him a few dates when the studio was free, but only if he was going to be more honest and transparent. Otherwise, what would be the point? I wrote this in a semi-joking, bro-to-bro tone, but I haven't heard back from Judd since, and he lives not far up the street from me. My naïveté in expecting him to seize this *incredible opportunity* was part of an ongoing narrative experienced with other actors I interviewed on the podcast, and this left me feeling, as usual, foolish and lost. But that was *my* problem, of course.

■ ■ ■

What happened with Judd Nelson wasn't necessarily a surprise. On the podcast, actors tended to present themselves very differently than filmmakers, writers and comedians did. The coy back-and-forth we often fell into could be charming, but it also made me wonder, as the host: Who was I talking to? A "real" person who happened to be an actor, or a replicant or a construct? My experience with Judd wasn't entirely unlike the one I recorded with Molly Ringwald earlier that year, even though we'd known each other since 1991, when she started dating a friend of mine, and we stayed in touch after they broke up. She accepted my invitation to appear on the podcast, though in retrospect I'm not exactly sure what she'd expected. I wanted to make her look good, as I do with all the guests, and came up with five or six topics I knew she could riff on, explaining how she felt and where she stood. And since I knew how opinionated and tough she could be when discussing Hollywood and her career in private I wanted her to feel comfortable enough on the air to open up. But a few days after we recorded the podcast, I heard that she'd been offended by some of my topics: Did she ever think that John Hughes had a sexual thing for her? What as a teenager was the true nature of her relationship with Warren Beatty? How did she deal with Robert Downey Jr.'s drug abuse while making *The Pick-Up Artist*?

Ultimately, she reached out and asked to talk through all this over dinner. We met at an upscale Italian restaurant in West Hollywood, where Molly relayed how she'd felt ambushed, that she wasn't in control and was being *used*. She thought some of the topics I'd brought up put her in an awkward position—things she would never want to talk about publicly, even though, I reminded her, while recording that session she'd candidly admitted to being called a "cunt" on Twitter by someone who didn't like an innocuous tweet she had posted—and that this was the moment she'd vowed to lay off Twitter. After a few glasses of wine we relaxed, and Molly said she simply disagreed with my approach and also that she was writing a memoir and couldn't afford to divulge *everything*—she had to save at least a few secrets. When two fans came up to our table and asked to take her photograph on their phone, Molly politely declined in the packed and noisy restaurant, the traffic whirring behind us on busy Third Street because this was a private moment.

■ ■ ■

I first noticed this reluctance among actors to be transparent with James Van Der Beek, of all people: a friend of mine, but also someone with whom I'd been working on a TV project and who also happened to have starred in *The Rules of Attraction*, based on my second novel. I wanted to do a podcast with James about the making of that movie and he enthusiastically agreed. He then mentioned that he was sick of the business and had decided to shuck the acting nonsense (this was before he was hired by CBS to costar in *CSI: Cyber*) and concentrate solely on writing and directing. He needed to air some complaints he had about where Hollywood was going, and about the failures of his own career—and he did so, to a degree, but for the most part, the angry and critical, pissed-off and disillusioned James I knew never appeared in the podcast. He was careful, respectful and, by the end, was worried whether he'd offended anyone—maybe he shouldn't have made that innocuous aside about James Franco? When my producer and I assured him he hadn't, James was visibly relieved. Should I have been surprised when an actor enacted a version of himself far more carefully than any civilian would? A version he'd want to *play* in front of an audience? No, that shouldn't have surprised me because *most* of us now are way more careful about how we present ourselves than ever before. What my podcast was fighting, I realized, was the limitations of the new world order. And even if this might be the new status quo, I still wanted to know: What the fuck was everybody protecting? Later, I would come to understand, it was the corporation.

One of the more labored podcasts I recorded was with Jason Schwartzman. Before we started he warned me that he was just generally a very angry person, so I should be prepared if he decided to rip loose, but this anger was nowhere to be found the first time we recorded. Instead, tired after having been up all night with a new baby, Jason struggled to engage and often asked if we could come back to a particular question after taking a break. And once we got to the second half of the podcast, it seemed that I was talking far more than my guest was. When the hour was over, Jason apologized that this wasn't the right day for him to be recording and said he felt genuinely terrible that he'd given so many of my questions only confused and perfunctory answers. I disagreed and told him the podcast was fine (plus after my producer's edit it would run more smoothly) but he insisted on retaping it a week later, when he promised to be better "prepared"—as if being "prepared" instead of just being himself was the point. And so we taped another session and edited the two into what we hoped was a more coherent whole. Yet Jason never came off as angry—in fact, one listener noted that he used the words "amazing" and "incredible" thirty-eight times when describing people he'd worked with over the last two decades, and that he kept everything humming with a positive and respectful vibe. Again, it was naïve of me to have expected anything else, but this new cautiousness and obsession with coming off as likable was happening everywhere. Even the porn star James Deen was more diplomatic talking about the behavior of his costar in a movie he and I had done together (Lindsay Lohan in *The Canyons*) than he had been in private. Like Judd Nelson, he reserved his only moment of public anger for a journalist, David Lipsky, who had attempted, James thought, to defame him.

■ ■ ■

In the late 1980s, when Tom Cruise and I lived in the same building in downtown New York, I saw him only twice—both times in the elevator. These brief sightings became the basis for a scene in *American Psycho* in which Patrick Bateman rides up in one with Cruise in a fictional apartment building on the Upper West Side, and though it can be argued that much of the novel is a madman's fantasy, the Tom Cruise I wrote into it was definitely based on reality. I wrote that scene in 1989, a year before Cruise was pictured romping in the Pacific on a *Rolling Stone* cover that I was to become overly invested in. Cruise was only twenty-seven in 1989 (I was twenty-five) but already such a generational icon that I thought including him would grant the novel a jolt of surreal authenticity. By July 1990, the summer of that *Rolling Stone* cover, Cruise was entering the next stage of his power. He'd already done all the stuff necessary to get there: propping up two old-timers (Paul Newman in *The Color of Money*, Dustin Hoffman in *Rain Man*) and helping them win Oscars; surviving a fiasco that was a bomb (*Legend*), and another that became a big hit (*Cocktail*), the movie that Bateman and Cruise discuss in

American Psycho, though Bateman thinks it's called *Bartender*; and proving he could play a showy, complicated role boldly and with no apologies (*Born on the Fourth of July*). The *Rolling Stone* cover was shot by Herb Ritts and suggests sex, of course, but the image of Cruise emerging from the foamy water also hints at rebirth, a new beginning, and that's where I thought I was heading as well after completing *American Psycho* at the end of 1989.

In the movie Cruise was promoting, *Days of Thunder*, he plays the race-car driver Cole Trickle and opens the picture in a burst of self-parody—racing a motorcycle wearing sunglasses and a swanky mullet, zooming through a sheet of fog while synthesized drumbeats herald his arrival. The movie was supposed to be a commercial for NASCAR, but what's odd is that despite his trademark intensity, Cruise is weightless here; he has no authority or charm, yet everyone bows to him and reacts immediately to everything he says and does, which makes them all seem crazy. It's shot with the impersonality of a Coke commercial, and the whole thing suggests the decadence of a very distant movie era. Cruise looks as pretty as a model but he can't loosen up, staying so clenched that not even Robert Towne—the legendary screenwriter, and slumming here—can liven him up with practical jokes and a few funny lines. *Days of Thunder* didn't work in the summer of 1990, and this would be one of the last times Cruise would command a film from beginning to end; it's also the only movie of his where he receives story credit. In 1990, we were still in the moment when few could foresee what a polarizing figure Tom Cruise would become. There was something so innocent and white and distinctly American about him: the seminary student from Syracuse who'd already married and divorced an older actress was now the biggest movie star in the world, showing off his abs on the cover of *Rolling Stone* in a wet T-shirt.

He was enigmatic yet still approachable—the grin hadn't hardened into granite, the hyena laugh wasn't so forced or pronounced and nobody was talking about Scientology. He seemed energetic, perpetually youthful, ambitious and unworried. He was living the collective dream of his era. There was no possibility this boy was going to become the least open and most secretive of movie stars—which would, for a time, make him the most fascinating. This guardedness (or insecurity), when it arrived, might have come from so many places. Was it the absent dad? (In a career spanning almost forty years Cruise has played a father only three times, including *Eyes Wide Shut*, incidentally a masterpiece.) Was it the dyslexia? Or the gay rumors he still hasn't erased? With no answers from the man himself, we can only guess. In many respects Cruise has never really shaken off that image captured by Ritts on that beach: the moment when our culture equated boyishness with ambiguous masculinity. *American Gigolo* was certainly a key influence for this, too, and photographers like Ritts and Bruce Weber also created an "ideal" that has been prevalent in the media ever since: they took standard teenage (and gay) boy pinups and eroticized them further with an artsy and ironic sheen. Cruise was one of the first movie stars to embody this and to help carry it forward—probably because he possibly was the least manly major actor of his generation. Though he belongs to an entirely different one, compare the forty-three-year-old Cruise in *War of the Worlds* to Gene Hackman in *The Conversation* at the same age.

Cruise never really erased the persona of the sexy-geek boy toy he played in *Risky Business*, and since time often freezes the occasion when an actor becomes a star, we'll have that initial image of him in our collective head forever. Was the summer of 1990 the beginning of this realization for him, when the excitement fades and is replaced by a horrible understanding that you're in fact a *thing* shaped by the mood of the public, and that celebrity is a business? He looks happy on the cover of *Rolling Stone*—coming off an amazing run, having recently met his future wife Nicole Kidman—but is this when he starts thinking, *Yes, I'm on a beach being shot by Herb Ritts, which is going to emphasize my physical attractiveness, and the purpose of this is to sell a movie that everyone involved with must know isn't very good?* Maybe this is the reason that all Cruise can offer here is adolescent beauty. We don't learn anything about him in the article that accompanies those pictures, and perhaps this is when the gossip and innuendo begin swirling around him. Rereading the profile many years later, I'm struck again by how little is revealed—how prefabricated it all seems, how obsessed Cruise is with maintaining his image and likability. I find myself thinking about how differently that elevator scene in *American Psycho* might be played today. Would Bateman, a man also obsessed with appearances, recognize a kindred soul? Or—after witnessing the couch jumping on *Oprah*, the hectoring on the *Today* show, the thing called *Vanilla Sky*, the *Going Clear* documentary and hearing about the Scientology allegations, the two divorces and "the auditions" for new wives, *The Mummy*—would Bateman quietly back away, hoping to go unnoticed?

■ ■ ■

In 2006, I moved back to Los Angeles to work on an adaptation of *The Informers*, a collection of short stories I'd published in 1994.

And, for the first time in nearly twenty years, I found myself in close proximity to actors simply because so many of them were involved in my work as a writer and a producer who also assisted in the casting of movies. Due to a certain desperation that many actors carry yet try hard to mask, I felt more empathy for them than I ever imagined I could, and I was sometimes empathic to a fault, occasionally to my own detriment. I often socialized with them and, on more than one occasion, hooked up. Once or twice I tried to help an actor more than I perhaps should have, because I'd been seduced and fallen for a performer whose agenda I should have seen more clearly. After arriving back in LA I'd been warned by a few industry veterans that this was part of the game in Hollywood, but it was one I'd never played before. When I was told not to get too seriously involved with an actor, I didn't listen. I preferred to have my ego stroked, and because of a kind of perverse sexual gratification that accompanied the seduction, I got tripped up.

The sex wasn't necessarily real, but then what was? We spent a year of preproduction to build what would cost millions of dollars (*The Informers* budget crested out at twenty million) and require a crew of hundreds, with locations stretching from Beverly Hills to Uruguay, and it was all something manufactured—a fantasy, an illusion. The stories the movie was based on were made up, my twenty drafts of the screenplay were an endless work of fiction, amounting to a complicated mosaic, that was futilely rigorous in its attempt to encompass eight fake storylines about imaginary people (and which ultimately bore little resemblance to the seriously compromised final product). Because of the large cast, the auditions alone took almost a year, so I was, in effect, dealing with hundreds upon hundreds of actors who wanted to play the four college-aged men at the center of the movie, and who were desperately persuasive about getting themselves cast. Interesting and unexpected things happened—I found out there was a wide array of possibilities, of a kind that I'd always suspected was just another Hollywood myth.

In retrospect, whatever pain I suffered was entirely my own fault, because I'd failed to play the game correctly and as a writer took everything too seriously (one of the actors nicknamed me "Dramatic Chipmunk," referring to a meme that was making the rounds in 2006). As the writer, I was trying to keep everything real outside the moviemaking process, and I mistakenly thought the process *itself* was real, despite the fact that we were making a *movie*. I assumed the deranged optimism a movie—that *fantasy*—required wouldn't spill out into the real and pragmatic worlds outside this realm. But you find out about a lot of things the hard way when you're making a movie, any movie. Maybe the director has sold himself as being more connected to the material than he actually is because he needs the money. Maybe one of the actors with a druggy past isn't as clean as you all thought (one of the stars of *The Informers* would die a month after the wrap party of a heroin overdose). Or maybe that actor you've become intimate with is only that: an actor longing to be a part of this fantasy, part of the family it takes to realize it, even if all the while he's just playing a role. The mutual degradation that revealed itself to me was a kind of absurd Hollywood joke without a punch line, one that, years later, I'm thankful for. On certain days, in certain situations, the memory of that time serves as a reminder of the struggles and disappointments that come with making a movie, and this momentary distraction can make me cringe, until I get my bearings and am able to shakily regroup. Of course the actors had warned me, and I hear them clearly now, but in order for the fantasy of it all to move forward this part had to be played very well; the seduction had to seem real so I could buy into a fantasy that I thought was real, and to allow the process to complete itself. In the end, these actors never got the role, no matter how hard I tried.

s e c o n d s e l f

I began making notes for *American Psycho* in the last week of December 1986 and started outlining it in the early spring of 1987, after I'd moved to New York and was about to rent a condo on Thirteenth Street—in a building previously noted for the fact that Tom Cruise lived there, even though the East Village was considered a semi-desolate area. Today, ten-million-dollar apartments are on the market in the same area, but this was unthinkable in 1987, when multicolored crack vials littered the streets like confetti, and Union Square—only a block away—was still a barren park favored largely by junkies, even as it was gradually gentrifying due in part to the Zeckendorf Towers, which had recently gone up across from it, and Danny Meyer's Union Square Cafe on Sixteenth Street was becoming the most popular restaurant in Manhattan. New York was—for some people—at the end of an era and at the beginning of a new one. My first day in the condo was April 1, the same day that the memorial service for Andy Warhol was held at St. Patrick's Cathedral, and that's also when *American Psycho* opens.

The first chapter's title, "April Fools," hints that what one is about to read isn't an exactly reliable narrative, that maybe it's all a dream, the collective sensibility of consumerist yuppie culture seen through the eyes of a deranged sociopath with a tenuous grip on reality. And maybe this is what the book became as I began writing it in 1987, because I was living in a kind of dreamworld, too—the surrealism I was experiencing personally mutating back into the fictional domain of Patrick Bateman. I didn't talk about this during or after the controversy the novel caused in 1991; only in the last few years, starting with that international book tour I grudgingly went through in 2010, have I admitted that on so many levels Patrick Bateman was me, at least while I was working on the book. We shared an illusory and distant relationship with a world that appalled us, yet we both wanted to connect with it. We felt disgusted by the society that had created us, as well as a resistance to what was expected of us, and we were infuriated by the idea that there was nowhere else to go. Patrick says, at one point, "I want to fit in," and he does and he doesn't. In 1987 this was also true for me.

Once I was satisfied with the outline, I began writing in Patrick Bateman's present-tense voice—and my plans didn't change much over the roughly three years it took me to complete the book. It had been worked out to such a degree in advance because of the seeming randomness of Bateman's life, and part of this had to do with the fact that *American Psycho* was initially far more straightforward and earnest, with the lonely young yuppie Patrick Bateman starring in a realistic novel with no overt violence or pornography, a young man lost on Wall Street, seduced and trapped by the greed of an era. This book would have completed a kind of trilogy detailing youthful '80s Reagan-era excess that had begun with *Less Than Zero*, been continued by *The Rules of Attraction* and would have ended with Bateman at the end of the decade: passive, older, wiser, no longer with his fiancée, disillusioned as he left the company he'd worked at. To do what? He didn't know. He was just relieved to be leaving an environment he'd never felt a part of or had outgrown, like Clay at the end of *Less Than Zero* and Sean at the end of *The Rules of Attraction*. But this original idea for the novel changed in a flash.

■ ■ ■

During the spring of 1987 I had dinner with a group of guys, one who was the older brother of a Bennington classmate of mine and all of them working on Wall Street making what seemed like a lot of money for recent business school grads in their mid- to late twenties. During my initial research I'd grown frustrated by their evasions about what exactly they *did* for the companies where they worked—information I felt was necessary, and finally understood really wasn't. I was surprised by the desire instead to show off their crazily materialistic lifestyles: the Armani suits, the hip, outrageously priced restaurants they could get reservations at, the cool Hamptons summer rentals and, especially, their expensive haircuts and tanning regimens and gym memberships and grooming routines. I began to realize that the standard hallmarks of gay male culture had been appropriated by straight male culture with the emergence of the heterosexual male dandy, something that had begun with the popularity of GQ magazine and *American Gigolo* at the dawn of the '80s. The competition between these guys was overwhelming: the one-upmanship and bragging bordered at times on the threatening, and during this particular meal (the last one, it turned out) I suddenly decided—apropos of nothing in particular—that Patrick Bateman would be a serial killer.

Or would *imagine* himself to be. (I never knew if it was one or the other, which in turn made the novel compelling to write. Is the answer more interesting than the mystery itself? I never thought so.) I have no idea why I made this connection during that dinner, but it changed my conception of the book, and late in the spring of 1987—or was it early summer?—I began re-threading the outline. And once this decision was reached the book started to mirror the surreal quality of my life during that period. A haze had descended over me after moving to New York and the only clarity came when I was alone, working on the novel.

■ ■ ■

I floated through 1987 in the midst of a dreamlike narrative that was decidedly mine yet also felt completely disconnected, as if it belonged to someone else. Who was this well-known young American writer cruising through Manhattan with a best seller at the age of twenty-three, who was both too young and too savvy (growing up in LA I learned that you become adept at dealing with the media by not caring about the media), who was part of the newly minted *literary* Brat Pack, photographed at clubs and parties, enjoying a bachelor's existence, every door seemingly wide open to him? It was supposed to be an '80s win-win, a kind of fantasy, though my anxiety and doubt about nearly everything kept blooming out of control. I skimmed articles about Bret Easton Ellis. I saw his picture in newspapers and magazines. I read that he'd been seen at certain art openings and nightclubs with certain young movie stars of the moment (Robert Downey Jr.,

Judd Nelson, Nic Cage) and at certain trendy restaurants (with literary Brat Pack cohort Jay McInerney) and sometimes I might have been there (paparazzi pics proved I was) and other times I couldn't be sure: my author's photo might have been printed next to a story about a gallery opening or a Midtown movie premiere, but that didn't mean I was there. Sometimes just an RSVP was proof of my presence at an event whether I'd attended it or not. I often saw my name embedded in lists that confirmed I'd been somewhere when I knew, in fact, I hadn't. In a sense there were now two Brets—the private and the public—and 1987 was the year I realized they coexisted, which was how unusual my life as a twenty-three-year-old celebrity seemed to me. After *Less Than Zero*, I attended that small college in Vermont for one more year and then moved back to the house in Sherman Oaks with my mom and two sisters for another year after I'd graduated, so I hadn't been on a public stage until moving to New York. It's not even that I cared all that much about having a double, it was just a New Sensation, as INXS put it in their ubiquitous single that played out as a key track over the party life of the city in 1987.

■ ■ ■

In the early fall of that year I published a second novel that received okay reviews and had so-so sales, at least compared to that first best seller, yet there was a massive amount of hype and press as well as a huge book party in a hip new club on the Lower East Side. I spent the duration of it in the owner's office, suffering from an intense anxiety attack; I'd thrown up in the cab taking me to the party, due to nerves and a hangover after reinforcement drinks at Jams. That November the *Less Than Zero* movie was released to mediocre reviews and a middling box office, but there were celebrity-packed screenings and parties while the Bangles' "Hazy Shade of Winter," the first single from the film's soundtrack, boomed from MTV and radios everywhere as it charted at #2 on *Billboard.* And I felt disconnected, as if this was all happening to someone else—a feeling of profound separation and alienation had taken over, yet I smiled and pretended everything was simple and nice and that everyone liked me even though this was decidedly untrue. One Bret bought into the lie of it all; the other Bret was intensely aware that it was only that, a lie. I was probably too young to fully enjoy and accept what was going on, which in turn made me frustrated and angry. What was this society that had allowed me to flourish? Why didn't I trust it? Why did I want to escape it? Where else was there to go?

My life was distinctly unlike the lives of my friends, who'd graduated with me in June 1986 and now had jobs that required them to go to an office (1987 was a time when you could graduate from college, find a job and pay a reasonable rent *somewhere* in Manhattan, something unimaginable given the moated gated community it is now, filled with what seems like only rich people and tourists). I kept strict writing hours in the condo on Thirteenth Street, where I tried to adhere to a routine that mirrored that of my friends who worked nine to five—though sometimes instead of having lunch I would walk to a theater and watch a movie. Then I'd resume writing before meeting up for a cocktail party, dinner somewhere and a nightclub, probably Nell's; that's how our evenings usually rolled. And depending on what night it was and how much work needed to be completed the following day, maybe a little cocaine was involved, though of course it was never "a little cocaine" and before we knew it dawn was rising over the East River and friends had to head to work without having slept—another tiny line, another shot of vodka, one more cigarette. But we could do this at twenty-three and twenty-four and twenty-five because we had the requisite youthful stamina, so it never seemed like a big deal. Instead of exhausting, it seemed romantic.

■ ■ ■

I distinctly remember having lunch at the Odeon on a Monday afternoon in October 1987, after a lost weekend, with a friend who'd also barely slept for two days, both of us not only hungover but still clearly wasted. Why I was having lunch at the Odeon with my friend, who was also twenty-three, and why we were both wearing suits when only half awake from our runaway weekends, is now—thirty years later—completely beyond me, something from not a distant era but a distant *century.* Yet it seemed then that everyone wore suits; I rarely went anywhere without wearing one, and neither did most of the men I knew, and while at that lunch—we were probably drinking champagne, and I was probably on Klonopin—I remember telling my friend about the last time I'd been at the Odeon, a few weeks earlier, when I found myself sharing cocaine with Jean-Michel Basquiat (we were both wearing suits) downstairs in the men's restroom during a drunken dinner after a photo shoot for *Interview* magazine. Basquiat asked why there were so few black people in my first two novels and I said something about the casual racism of the white society I was depicting and we lit up cigarettes as we walked back, high, to the respective groups at our tables—just a typical encounter for me in the fall of 1987.

Sometime during our lunch my friend commented that people appeared to be getting up mid-meal and leaving their tables en masse. I hadn't noticed because my back was to the room, but when I looked over my shoulder I saw that young men in suits were hurriedly paying checks and dashing out onto West Broadway. We asked our waiter what was happening and he said it "seemed" the stock market was crashing. I very clearly remember him using that word—one of the few things I remember clearly at all from that period—on what was, in fact, Black Monday. My friend and I had nothing to do with the market and so we finished lunch, exhausted to the point of amusement, at one of the last tables occupied in the restaurant. And despite the shock of Black Monday, the market's collapse hardly affected the mind-set of young Manhattan during the few years that were left of the 1980s. If anything the decadence ramped up, as if to defy what Wall Street had told us, and perhaps this defiance was not an atypical response to that era.

■ ■ ■

My focus was the novel, which had become my only source of clarity during that period. I wrote the entire manuscript in the rented condo on Thirteenth Street, which had a futon mattress on the floor and some patio furniture scattered around, along with an elaborate stereo system that had an insanely expensive turntable, and a makeshift writing desk—not chicly minimalist, just empty; a place "decorated" by someone who couldn't be bothered, somebody easily distracted by everything else. The book was reliable and I wasn't, not necessarily. Away from the novel my life was a haze, and I can't say now with any certainty if I really was at a U2 concert at the Meadowlands with a couple of Wall Street guys in the spring of 1987, or at the premiere of *Dirty Dancing* that August, or maybe at the premiere of *Who's That Girl* earlier that summer, hanging out with Griffin Dunne. I remember Madonna's slightly ominous title track to that film wafting out of radios all summer long ("*Light up my life, so blind I can't see / light up my life, no one can help me now*") and I remember sitting in a packed theater at the opening-day matinee of Brian De Palma's *The Untouchables*, and later that year being at the same theater for *Fatal Attraction*. But was I backstage before a Def Leppard concert talking to lead singer Joe Elliott while he ate a vegan meal, or was that just part of the dream? By the end of the year, was Jay McInerney really dating a once-unknown model who'd become famous because of a knife attack that left her beautiful face glamorously slashed, and did I really accompany them on their first public appearance—was it at another movie premiere, maybe *Moonstruck*? Was the paparazzi mob so insistent on getting a picture of the new celebrity couple that my own companion was elbowed violently aside when we left the screening, and did she burst into tears, and was a massive bruise already beginning to form above her rib cage at the after party?

Did I actually visit the set of Oliver Stone's *Wall Street* sometime in April or May and even smoke a cigarette with Charlie Sheen between takes? I remember seeing the finished movie that

December at a screening back in Los Angeles when I was home for Christmas and thinking that the seduction of Sheen's Bud Fox by Michael Douglas's Gordon Gekko was the most powerful part of the movie. Because that seduction was happening to all of us then, sort of, and it was still playing out by the time the movie was released. But the second act offered redemption, which marred everything that made the first part of the movie feel so of the moment. The second half was the lie that never came true, that never played itself out on the real Wall Street, with the real Bud Foxes and the real Gordon Gekkos—because there never was any redemption. In some ways, I saw *American Psycho* as the surreal corrective, the logical outcome of where Bud Fox was heading in 1988 and 1989, even as I also realized that I was writing about a nightmare version of myself.

■ ■ ■

Once I'd adjusted to life in Manhattan I became more focused not just on the novel but also on juggling my own reality apart from the novel—or maybe I just got used to things. It could be my life calmed down and fell into a restful rhythm after the stressful excitement of that initial year of 1987 or maybe it was simply that the Klonopin I'd been prescribed by a bored shrink on the Upper East Side was helping. Possibly inhabiting Patrick Bateman had clarified things for me; as the novel grew darker post–Black Monday, I began to feel a release. Just as there had been two Brets, there were two Patrick Batemans: there was the handsome and socially awkward boy next door whose name no one could remember because he seemed like everybody else—having *conformed* like everybody else—and there was the nocturnal Bateman who roamed the streets looking for prey, asserting his monstrousness, his individuality. At the end of the '80s I saw this as an appropriate response to a society obsessed with the surface of things and inclined to ignore anything that even hinted at the darkness lurking below. The novel seemed an accurate summation of the Reagan era, with the Iran-Contra affair being obliquely referenced in the last chapter, and the violence unleashed inside was connected to my frustration, and at least hinted at something real and tangible in this superficial age of surfaces. Because blood and viscera were real, death was real, rape and murder were real—though in the world of *American Psycho* maybe they weren't any more real than the fakery of the society being depicted. That was the book's bleak thesis.

■ ■ ■

If I remembered little of 1987 in New York, then all I now remember about 1988 and 1989 is working on the book. I know that Basquiat died less than a year after our conversation in the men's room at the Odeon; I know that I met someone I ended up living with for seven years, a Wall Street lawyer a few years older than I was, closeted and from the South, who sometimes reminded me of Patrick Bateman and sometimes didn't; I know that I eventually made a half-hearted attempt at decorating the apartment on Thirteenth Street after purchasing it; I know that I finished *American Psycho* in December 1989, almost three years to the date after I began it; I know that it was finally released in March 1991 after the initial publisher canceled it. And I now know that many people from that period assumed after it was published that my career as a writer was over. I now know that I was never happier than I was in the summer of 1991.

post-sex

As a Gen Xer, finding my father's *Playboy* stash in the bottom cabinet of his nightstand in the house on Valley Vista in the early 1970s was my first gateway into the world of nudity and sexual imagery. Despite what would become my preferences, the nudity in *Playboy* was intensely fascinating because I had nothing else to compare it to; a few illustrations in the copy of *The Joy of Sex* my parents kept in their closet could be powerfully erotic but they were only drawings, and the photographs in *Playboy* were tactile and alive with the color of flesh. And there were sometimes nude men in the *Playboy* layouts (merely decorative and never the main attraction) as well as in the stills from their annual Sex in Cinema roundup. *Playboy* was my introduction to the idea of the male gaze (and, later, *Penthouse* and *Oui*), while I lay on the green shag carpet next to the king-size waterbed in the groovy San Fernando Valley of the mid-1970s. In a pre-AIDS society where sexuality was discussed casually and without any anxiety or menace, the body was free of all signifiers except pleasure. There was no fear or dread in sexual imagery yet—no irony. It was, I've realized increasingly as I've gotten older, an innocent time, even though we decidedly felt it wasn't as we lived through it.

This was an era in which magazines were the *only* way to find sustained images of nudity. Though there was nudity in American movies in the 1970s, you had to have cable and then *time* the movie in order to catch the nudity or soft-core sex scene you'd originally seen in a theater and wanted to watch again when you were, um, alone. (This happened many times with the sex scene in *Looking for Mr. Goodbar* with Diane Keaton and Richard Gere, which I watched over and over on the Z Channel.) We were still years away from the advent of DVR, and VHS cassettes weren't ubiquitous yet, and porn was still exclusively shown in theaters, and so we could see images of naked people only by getting our hands on a *magazine*. For many of us boys (and girls) this portal into the world of nudity was usually our father's *Playboy*, or maybe later our mother's *Playgirl* (though this was decidedly more rare), at least until we were old enough to buy magazines that were usually far more explicit than anything *Playboy* had initially offered.

■ ■ ■

In this age of the nude selfie, of porn spam and the freedom to find every kind of sex act available on your phone within seconds, it's hard to remember when nudity was still taboo, private, secret, between covers, and you had to pay for it. Or that pictures with posed models were actually *exciting*—images that raised the temperature and got things going in a way they simply don't anymore for most of us, and these photos were our introduction to a deeper world of pornography and actual sex. As I got older, *Playboy* stopped becoming the go-to for masturbatory fantasies, and I began buying more explicit stuff at newsstands even though at fourteen or fifteen I was nowhere near the legal age. Maybe I looked older, or perhaps the vendors didn't care; sometimes I'd wear a leather jacket and sunglasses to make myself look more adult, but I was never asked for ID in the LA of the late 1970s. *Hustler* was a favorite of mine because men were included in many of Suze Randall's elaborate pictorials, and it was also popular with everyone else because *Hustler*, unlike *Playboy* then, showed pink. There was also a moment when *Hustler*, and *Penthouse*, in its Forum letters section, flirted with—and endorsed—male bisexuality, at least until AIDS slammed that door shut.

And the next gateway I passed through was when I saw my first pornographic film: I was in the ninth grade and a wealthy friend who lived in Bel Air (his father owned a football team) had a sleepover and through some vague connections had obtained a VHS copy of a recently produced porn movie. The film felt incredibly taboo—and that night so transgressive that forty years later I can still remember the pattern in the massive bedroom's wallpaper that lined the second floor of the mansion my friend lived in. Even at fourteen (try imagining now a fourteen-year-old boy who has never seen porn before) I knew it was terrible—unattractive performers, poorly shot, edited by a sloth—but it still offered a jolt, and I understood that I had now crossed into another world with no looking back. It wasn't until we were mobile Southern California boys at fifteen and sixteen, with cars at our disposal, that we began obtaining and trading cassettes like contraband—and I use that word because at a certain point the availability was so fraught with frustration and difficulty, and there were so many impasses, that these tapes were surprisingly hard to come by. Our needs demanded an incredible amount of sheer will and planning, but the testosterone-crazed energy of adolescent sexuality helped us get what we desired so badly, and the hunt itself was also part of the pleasure.

Some '70s feminists complained about *Playboy*, and porn in general, and as males we were confused: What was wrong about looking at and objectifying beautiful women (or men)? What was wrong about this gender-based instinct to stare and covet? Why shouldn't this be made more easily available to horny boys? And what was wrong with the idea of the male gaze? Leaving aside everything we now know about toxic masculinity (whatever that is), no ideology will ever change these basic facts that are ingrained by a biological imperative. Why should we be turning away from our sexuality? My male friends often wondered, *Who is empowered here? It's certainly not me. I'm staring at this beautiful woman I desperately want and who I'll probably never meet.* That was the majority teen-boy feeling, which intensified the fantasy of it all; doesn't this slight sense of punishment and disdain overlaying the enjoyment always add to the experience? The feminist reaction to *Playboy* seemed unfair because our options pre-internet were so severely limited—maybe a couple issues of a magazine per *month*—that to apply moral criticism to our desires seemed cruel.

■ ■ ■

Today the idea of actually going to a store (Le Sex Shoppe was our usual stop in the San Fernando Valley) and *renting* or buying porn and having that be the only source for a month is unthinkable and impractical, yet in that long-gone world it's how men dealt with the need to obtain sexual images—and since they were so rare we imbued them with a deeper meaning and perhaps made them more powerful and erotic than they actually were. Then, in the late 1980s and into the '90s, DVDs soon gave way to the incredible array of pornography on the internet, and I marveled at the amount of choice that was so effortlessly available, compared to what there'd been available in my adolescence and twenties. And yet this abundance changed my relationship to nudity and porn: it made it more commonplace, and somewhat less exciting, just as ordering a book from Amazon was less exciting than walking into a bookstore and browsing for an hour or so, or purchasing shoes online instead of heading to the mall and trying on a pair of Top-Siders while interacting with a salesperson, or buying a record at Tower, or actually standing in line for a movie you wanted to see. This cooling of excitement on all levels of the culture has to do with the disappearing notion of *investment*.

When you went to a bookstore or record store or movie theater or newsstand, you took the time to invest a greater amount of effort and attention in these various expeditions than you would by clicking a few buttons—effort and attention that were tied to a deeper attempt to connect with the LP, the hardcover, the film, the porn. You had a rooting interest in enjoying the experience because you'd invested—and were more likely to find gratification because of this. The idea of dismissing a book after five pages on your Kindle, turning off a movie in its first ten minutes after buying it on Apple or not listening through a whole song on Spotify wasn't an option—why do that after you'd driven to the Sherman Theater on Ventura Boulevard, the Crown Books in Studio City, the Tower Records on Sunset, the newsstand on Laurel Canyon? But what happens when things are almost *automatically* available—when a novel or a song or a movie or a naked woman or five naked women or a naked woman engaged in an orgy with five hung men is only a click away? When nudity and the idea of sexual gratification become so routine you can instantly hook up with someone and see naked pics of that soon-to-be sex partner within seconds, an exchange as casual as ordering a book on Amazon or downloading a new release on Apple—then this lack of investment renders everything the same. If everything's available without any effort or dramatic narrative whatsoever, who cares if you like it or if you don't? And the pulse-pounding excitement—the *suspense*—of the effort you once put into *finding* erotic imagery has now been lost with the lo-fi ease of accessibility, which in fact has changed our experience of *expectation*. There was a romance to that analog era, an ardency, an otherness that is missing in the post-Empire digital age where everything has ultimately come to feel disposable.

■ ■ ■

In the fall of 2014, while I watched *The Imitation Game*, director Morten Tyldum's film about the genius Alan Turing, my interest began to fade and was replaced by a low-level annoyance when I started thinking: Haven't we moved past such an old-fashioned, antiquated notion about gay victimization—including this ultimate gay-martyr movie? I flashed on my experience of reading Andrew Hodges's *Alan Turing: The Enigma* when I was in college—a book that appealed to the gay men I knew not necessarily because of what Turing had accomplished as a code breaker during the Second World War, but because of Turing's homosexuality—at least that's what got them interested in the book initially. The divide between the real Alan Turing and the role Benedict Cumberbatch played was distracting since Turing, while in many respects a victim of his times, never really considered himself a victim. He was in all probability a much more nuanced, contradictory and complicated man than the desperate, helpless, fumbling, lovable guy that Harvey Weinstein and company were trying to sell. Turing was a genuine weirdo who often knowingly or unknowingly victimized *himself*, yet the movie's victim narrative makes this his defining characteristic. *The Imitation Game* offers a dark story with a suicide looming at the end, but in typical Weinstein fashion it's turned into a rousing acclamation of the human spirit: Alan Turing might have killed himself, but in the film's triumphant ending we learn that without his genius (and, of course, his sacrifice) we never would've had the computer or artificial intelligence or the microwave or video games and so on—and moviegoers can walk out feeling good about themselves. And yet *The Imitation Game* has at its center a brilliant and intellectually sophisticated gay man, something that's rare to nonexistent in current cinema anywhere, and it was a movie made for a *mass* audience, not just the art house. It did quite well financially ($230 million worldwide) because it's about problem-solving and *not* gay consciousness.

■ ■ ■

Watching *The Imitation Game* made me think about Andrew Haigh's 2011 breakthrough *Weekend* and I wistfully wondered while leaving the theater, *What happened? Weren't there supposed to be more movies like* Weekend *at this stage in the game?* Written and directed by Haigh, it depicts two young men who meet in a gay bar in a city outside of London on a Friday night—just a casual hookup with neither of them the other's preferred choice. Russell (played by Tom Cullen) is quiet, guarded, self-conscious, a loner, while Glen (Chris New) is more comfortable in his skin, open and angry, and prone to shaking up the gay status quo; he's confrontational and likes to stir up trouble. They're both attractive, but not in the stereotypical manner that gay media generally espoused (at least in 2011), meaning they aren't *personalities* and they're not—in that lingo—*camp*. These are just two guys who meet, are sexually attracted to each other, go to bed together and wake up in Russell's apartment on Saturday morning. And so begins, in its quiet, somewhat muted but lyrical style, the movie that generations of gay men had been waiting for: simply about guys who find out things about each other without becoming role models for anyone or anything. They fuck (explicitly), drink, do drugs and admit their frustrations about gay life, and this guileless movie appears to have no overt agenda.

I remember the tension this caused during a first viewing before it was officially released: after decades of terribly earnest queer cinema was this actually going to be a story we hadn't seen told so simply before, about two men who—in less than forty-eight hours—make a deep connection with each other and fall in love? Yes, the movie says, it is, and maybe that's what a lot of movies could be about from now on. Gay men had never been portrayed like this. As we watch Russell and Glen talking and occasionally arguing, we begin to see something rarely depicted this intelligently in movies, whatever their sexual orientation: the opening of consciousness, a study in contrasts, two people changing their minds, their once fervent system of beliefs now subtly shifting because they're falling in love. There's no camp here, no gay signifiers; the men are resolutely lower-middle-class and nonfabulous, there's no melodrama or hysterics, and yet nothing that's butch or bro. The movie isn't mumblecore, exactly, nor is it done in a cheap neorealist style—the very good dialogue is obviously *written*, and it's beautifully shot on digital video, lo-fi and naturalistic with casually stunning compositions and a rich warm glow. It ends on a railway platform in a train station in Nottingham on a Sunday afternoon with one of them going away, heading to the United States for two years, and it's quite possible these men might never see each other again. The ending, like the rest of the movie, doesn't lurch toward dramatic hyperbole or ideology, and it becomes wrenching in its *refusal* to hype or sell anything; there is no agenda. It's just a sexy, funny, sad movie.

There is nothing cute or lovable or tragic about *Weekend* and it doesn't succumb to the PSA banality of so much of bad queer cinema floating around the festival circuit. The reviews were good—people caught what this movie was doing—and yet in *The New Yorker* Richard Brody slammed what he called "the bland sentimentality and dull attitudinizing" that turns "the movie into an empty frame of good intentions." The key words here are "bland" and "dull"—but for a generation of gay men these qualities amount to a loud wake-up call, indicating that movies about gay men don't need to have an explicit ideology or dramatic agenda—it's just cinema, it's just art. The good intentions of *Weekend* are exactly what Brody finds frustrating: these are simply people, not stand-ins for some impossibly noble ideal that the corporate gay community longs for and embraces—that upbeat and (yes) bland role model in which everything's constantly experienced through the lens of identity politics and ideology, and with rules on how people should express themselves within a certain range of propriety. Some in that adamant community took issue with *Weekend* at initial screenings—according to IFC, who released it—and wished the movie had been more "gay positive," worrying whether the guys were using condoms and concerned about the amount of weed they smoked, and the beer they drank, and cocaine they shared on Saturday night—on top of which they actually disagreed (blasphemy alert) about the importance of gay marriage. It seemed that some in the smiling corporate gay community blindly refused to understand the movie on its own terms. As A. O. Scott wrote in *The New York Times*, "*Weekend* is about the paradoxes and puzzlements of gay identity in a post-identity-politics era." The shock of *Weekend* is that there is no political cause at the heart of it.

■ ■ ■

Chilliness, coldness, remoteness, distance, austerity, minimalist: these are words that can apply to the styles of some of the greatest filmmakers, the ones who operated with a God's-eye neutrality. This doesn't mean their movies lacked passion, but rather that they relayed their vision of the world without emotional hyperbole or the kinds of aggressive editorializing that Hollywood largely favors over subtlety and indirection. The very nature of the medium encourages bigness, momentum, the expansive flourish and visual spectacle—why make a movie if it has no style?—and there are the rare filmmakers who fused the two, managing to be both emotionally indirect *and* grand: Hitchcock, Antonioni, Kubrick. But for the most part restraint doesn't really play in mainstream American filmmaking or even in the American vernacular; it's an aesthetic our filmmakers have rarely embraced. Yet the very notion of looking at things you shouldn't be seeing—and most movies are narratives about secrets—itself implies a passive, voyeuristic approach to one's subjects, and this is reflected in how an audience watches a film: as passive observers.

Sometimes this smoothness, calmness and distance, this remove and lack of sentiment, is really the essence of the voyeuristic experience. The camera can either editorialize and force you into certain feelings or play it entirely differently by showing things neutrally and ask *you* to bring something to the picture, which might, for example, have a complicated and contradictory character or a morally ambiguous nature at its center that the movie isn't going to simplify or resolve for you. Sometimes these are the movies that offer the greatest pleasure when you aren't swept along by a tide of forced feelings but carried away by their indirection and style, responding to the mood and atmosphere, rather than the more obvious components you find in most American movies—the overemphatic screenplay, for instance. But that's not to say those movies aren't also enjoyable; I've loved certain Spielberg movies though not in the same way I love an Antonioni or Bergman or Godard or Rohmer movie. Hitchcock's greatness often lies in how cold and daunting he can be—so cruel and withholding. That kind of emotional austerity can end up moving you as powerfully as a truly sappy love story. Kubrick's *Barry Lyndon* displays the hallmarks of this approach: the visual beauty is staggering; the director's control is as hypnotic as is his showmanship; and the main character is remote, cold and unlikable, as he holds center stage for three hours. Yet this overview of his character yields greater dividends than it would have if Kubrick had opted for something more emotionally conventional or overtly comical—if he'd gone all *Tom Jones* in his adaptation of Thackeray's comedy of manners. The remoteness of *Barry Lyndon* is what gives it an alienated majesty.

▪ ▪ ▪

In the fall of 2016 I happened to see two movies back-to-back, randomly, for no other reason than they opened on the same Friday, and this inadvertent pairing seemed instructive, since *Moonlight* was written and directed by a straight man (Barry Jenkins) and *King Cobra* by a gay man (Justin Kelly). I don't believe that only gay people should direct gay-themed films (many of them absolutely shouldn't) but in the case of a film like *Moonlight* that is, at heart, about gay male desire—the whole thing hinges on this, its third act completely dependent on it—the result strikes one at times as the strained progressive attempt of a straight artist to present a particular notion of what it's like to be gay. The actual visual depiction of desire in *Moonlight* is pretty much nonexistent, and in the few flashes of it the movie seems obviously not the work of a gay sensibility—by which I mean, basically, the dude-on-dude gaze—and this undermines the movie for me. In effect, the entertainment press lionized it not because it was a great film but because it checked off every box in our current obsession with identity politics. The main character was gay, black, poor, bullied and a victim.

The aesthetics of *King Cobra* aren't as fancy literary as *Moonlight*, yet its ideology is more interesting on a certain level because *King Cobra* tells a true-crime story whose lead characters just happen to be gay within all its crazy real-life drama, and it's not about bullying or victimization or marginalization or inclusivity, all things many of us don't respond to in American movies. (Give us dancing! Give us bank heists! Give us monsters! Give us spectacle!) In *Moonlight*, Chiron's a black kid who got a losing ticket in the birth lottery and grows up poor, whereas the gay white dudes in *King Cobra* are distinctly middle-class and therefore have more opportunities to squander their privilege, and they do so spectacularly. *Moonlight* is overly invested in Chiron's pain because without it the movie wouldn't exist—this is a victim narrative. Which isn't to say that people like Chiron—or the insecurity of black hypermasculinity, not to mention the enormous fragility of black life in general—don't exist, merely that their narratives tend to hit the same ideology, and that a filmmaker needs to work harder, perhaps, to uncover the volition in them. The teeming sexuality of *King Cobra*—and the business of gay masculine desire, the filming and selling and buying of it—is what gives the movie, for some of us, an urgent claim on our attention, a cinematic charge. Gay men as superficial capitalists driven to crime seemed to me, in that moment, a more progressive step in post-gay cinema than yet another anguished-victim scenario. Your white approval of *Moonlight* was supposed to make you feel virtuous. And while it's nice to feel virtuous, it's worth considering whether *feeling* virtuous and *being* virtuous are actually the same thing.

■ ■ ■

On a podcast I recorded, the actor Mark Duplass said that one reason he was glad to be a new member of the Academy of Motion Picture Arts and Sciences was so he could support "a movie like *Moonlight*," which was scheduled for release in a few weeks. I hadn't seen *Moonlight*, though Duplass, who is white and straight and liberal, seemed to echo a sentiment I'd picked up on social media, which already was supporting the movie unequivocally without many of its champions having seen it. A friend of mine, a black entertainment lawyer in Hollywood, hadn't seen *Moonlight* either, but as he sat down to dinner with me the night before it opened his excitement at seeing a big indie drama whose leading character was a queer black male was palpable. His blind enthusiasm reminded me of a heated debate we'd had over Ryan Coogler's 2013 movie *Fruitvale Station*. Aesthetically, I thought that film was sentimental—the *point* of it seemed to be everywhere, and there was an earnestness built into the retelling of this tragedy that made it the Sundance equivalent of a snuff movie about fate. Actually our positions weren't that far apart when looking at *Fruitvale Station* on an *aesthetic* level. His taste, like mine, runs to the grand flourishes that the cinema can offer and, like me, he prefers genre movies. But he admitted that *Fruitvale Station* had shaken him to the core because he so rarely saw a movie where a young handsome black man was just trying to get by and having to deal with all the hassles and burdens of just being black. So he found the final sequences of *Fruitvale Station*, when the protagonist, Oscar Grant, is casually shot and killed, completely overwhelming. Not necessarily because this was an artistically accomplished film, but because he could—even from his different class and background—relate to Grant and feel that a part of his own story was being told, and he couldn't stop choking up the day after he'd seen the movie. When he described this reaction, I began to see *Fruitvale Station* through his eyes. While the movie wasn't for me, I could understand how, apart from its aesthetics, my friend could be affected by it. I finally realized he'd had a similar experience to the one I'd had with *Weekend*, a movie that also ends on a train platform.

The difference, for me, was that I'd found the *aesthetics* of *Weekend* stronger: it was more understated, more neutral, its compositions more cinematic, the protagonists' innocence and victimization wasn't overly stressed, and the only thing they were victimized by was loneliness—and yes, they were also white. On social media people who rejected my reservations about *Fruitvale Station* seemed to suggest I should like it no matter what, hinting, in fact, that I was camouflaging my racism by quarreling about the *aesthetics* of the movie—which, considering its budget and ambitions, aren't by any means bad. And though I recognize that my aesthetic preferences, like everyone's, were created within the context of my own upbringing, they also rely on a set of criteria that don't answer exclusively to victimhood. But these social media critics wanted to imply that my whiteness was an *ideological* error, that my comfortable unawareness was an indisputable problem, yet I'd argue that living without a direct experience of poverty or state-sponsored violence, growing up without ever being presumed a guaranteed threat in public places and never facing an existence where protection is hard to come by don't equate to a lack of empathy, judgment, or understanding on my part and don't rightly and automatically demand my silence. But this is an age that judges everybody so harshly through the lens of identity politics that if you resist the threatening groupthink of "progressive ideology," which proposes universal inclusivity except for those who dare to ask any questions, you're somehow fucked. Everyone has to be the same, and have the same reactions to any given work of art, or movement or idea, and if you refuse to join the chorus of approval you will be tagged a racist or a misogynist. This is what happens to a culture when it no longer cares about art.

■ ■ ■

When did people start identifying so relentlessly with victims, and when did the victim's worldview become the lens through which we began to look at everything? Why was *Moonlight* so inordinately drawn to the character Chiron, whom we see at three different stages of his life over the course of the movie: child, adolescent and man, each in a separate section? Because, born poor to a drug-addicted mother and an absent father, he's a victim all the way through—and so here we are in American indie movies' favorite scenario. The movie asks us to endure Chiron's pain without offering us much of anything else. There's nothing particularly interesting or admirable about Chiron, so the only thing at stake is his sadness and pain. He's not into anything—not music or poetry or comic books—and is simply a cipher. And because of this *Moonlight* seems to like its bullying scenes, climaxing when Chiron gets beat up by a schoolmate, most of all, and this is when the movie becomes active instead of passive and Barry Jenkins is strongest and most direct as a filmmaker. The movie is an elegy to pain, bursting with one feel-bad moment after another, a litany of rejections. Movies have always depicted suffering, of course, but there's a new kind of suffering that contemporary audiences are enthralled by, and seem to overidentify with, and that's suffering caused by victimization. Sometimes Jenkins doesn't make a big deal out of this and that's when *Moonlight* works best—as visual mosaic, casual and loose. At other times the violins and cellos and oboes start swooning over the soundtrack to signal a more aspirational and high-minded movie, and sometimes the movie feels too pristinely well-intentioned, wanting you to admire its style and good taste, and yet it badly needs more humor, more lightness, more sexual flash. The whole experience is dour and downbeat, and it fails to understand that those two distinct styles could coexist, or that we'd be more interested in Chiron if there was a fighter in him. But the movie has little interest in making him a stronger character. Chiron's mostly an enigma and *Moonlight* is curiously fascinated with him as a chaste, beautiful, sad-eyed angel.

This chasteness reveals a hetero sensibility at work in *Moonlight*, specifically in relation to how gay male desire is portrayed. Not that *Moonlight* needed to go all Gregg Araki but the movie has no sexual heat, and apart from the bullying it sidesteps scenes by overstylizing them for fear they might be too upsetting for an audience. When Chiron's mother screams at him as a little boy and calls him a "faggot" we don't hear the word, but only lip-read it, and the scene is further stylized by playing in slow motion with music ladled over it, and this distance lessens our experience of his pain, and the scene seems evasive, as if this primal gay-boy-versus-mother scene is something the straight filmmaker simply didn't comprehend. A group of schoolboys gather together and compare dick size—yet the scene goes nowhere. Of course you could argue that's just the movie's style: elliptical and noncommittal. But many opportunities to depict gay desire are missed, as others are elsewhere in what turns out to be a very mild movie. *Moonlight* makes it easy for certain straight and black audiences to respond to it by removing actual gay sex from the equation, and this bargain comes at a high price aesthetically.

I think this is why some audiences outside of the liberal Hollywood bubble apparently laughed at the movie. A few weeks after it opened, E. Alex Jung posted a piece on *Vulture* called "The Sad, Surreal Experience of Seeing an Audience Laugh at *Moonlight*." The writer cited the differences between watching the movie at a press screening, and then seeing it again with the public at the Brooklyn Academy of Music on a packed Friday night, and taking that audience to task for rejecting certain scenes and laughing at how some of them portrayed sexuality (or didn't). The writer was stunned, but I don't think the paying audience was wrong—this was their genuine reaction and if this seemed "sad" and "surreal" to the *Vulture* writer, obviously hoping the audience would conform to an ideology rather than respond to the film's aesthetics, then Jung had an out-of-touch bias against that audience. Why shouldn't a section of the paying audience feel however they want, or laugh whenever they like, at a movie that approaches everything evasively, or with such solemnity that they can't help but giggle at its self-seriousness and unwillingness to be up-front about shit? In the beach scene involving the teenaged Chiron and his classmate Kevin, the movie slows down and there's half a kiss—no tongue, skin, flesh, reciprocation—while Kevin gives Chiron a hand job. No matter how damaged and passive Chiron might be, this could have provided him, and the movie itself, with a chance to explode with awkward passion. And this might have scared Kevin, who we have assumed was straight until now, and laid the groundwork for the severe beating that comes later, which after two viewings, still makes no dramatic sense—only that the movie wants to show Chiron getting the shit beat out of him, and therefore continuing his victim narrative.

■ ■ ■

When we finally meet Chiron as an adult in the third section, it's ten years later, he's a somewhat successful drug dealer, yet he's almost as mute and sullen and inexpressive as he was when we last saw him. Wouldn't it have been a more "progressive" view if Chiron had defeated his old victimized self, if this big and beautiful black guy by then could have easily found physical intimacy and perhaps affection and maybe even love on the down-low? Maybe dissatisfied or unhappy, but that would have constituted a dramatic progression *and* an ideological triumph. Instead he's just a man-child who hasn't had sex since getting jerked off on that beach years before, and *Moonlight* wants us to believe the most chaste hand job in the history of movies had stunted this stud into celibacy. (If the boys had given each other blow jobs, I doubt the movie would have been as wildly acclaimed by the entertainment press, or won the Academy Award for Best Picture.) This is a literary conceit: the hand job that could never be forgotten. That the grown-up Chiron wouldn't, on the down-low, be satisfying his desires is also a literary fantasy—but this is part of the sullenness of the movie and underlies its basic conservatism as well, how proud it is of its values and what it represents, an Oprah experience. The movie's pulling punches, and I found it all slightly maddening: the scene in which the adult Chiron has a wet dream is caused by a brief montage of Kevin smoking a cigarette; maybe if it were the younger Kevin it might make sense, but since Chiron hasn't even *seen* the older Kevin at this point you wonder whom he's dreaming about. According to *Vulture*, audiences laughed at this sequence, too. As a gay man, something feels off to me about the chaste ending when Chiron goes back to Kevin's house after the reunion at the restaurant and then nothing happens. Forget sex, what about a kiss? No, instead of sex we get . . . a *hug*. When asked about this, Barry Jenkins said that what Chiron needs is "affection," not sex. Well, so the question becomes: Can't he have both? Aren't the two intertwined? Jenkin's answer is a straight man's answer, not a gay man's answer, and that's why the movie feels lopsided.

■ ■ ■

Certainly the entertainment press and a portion of the audience responded to *Moonlight* as a Black Lives Matter movie, and the strong, vibrant black bodies of the adult Chiron and the kindly, saintly drug dealer Juan, who took care of Chiron as a child, seemed to them a defiant rebuke to the endless parade of lifeless bodies of black men that we had seen in the media coverage of shooting after shooting. With so many black men having been killed that year, one understands the enormity of the weight that was placed on *Moonlight*'s fragile shoulders in that moment. *Moonlight* portrayed a *different* kind of man, one we hadn't seen in movies (like Russell and Glen in *Weekend*, for some of us), and many saw this as new and something to be celebrated. To some extent it was, just as *Weekend* was, but—on both aesthetic and ideological grounds—is replacing the thug with the oversensitive and victimized man-boy a sign of progress? The movie seemed almost like it was created to be idealized by our current media culture and by liberal Hollywood's fake-woke corporate culture. Chiron isn't difficult, he's not messy, and he's presented as being as squeamish about gay sex as the straight men in the audience perhaps are. The main character's rarity may have given the film something of a free pass, which allowed the media to overrate it, but it's strange to see *Moonlight* proclaimed—briefly, for maybe a year or two until revisionists take aim—a masterpiece. On one level, *Moonlight* is the *kind* of story that needs to be told yet the overprotective reaction to it (as the *Vulture* piece highlighted) could, of course, be seen as condescending as well.

■ ■ ■

A few years ago when a viewer complained to Shonda Rhimes, a top TV producer and showrunner, that there was too much gay sex on certain series she had created, Rhimes shot back, wagging her finger, that what people were seeing was not "gay sex" but simply "sex." Some of us scratched our heads—it was? As a man not neutered by his sexuality, when I look for pornography online I'm not typing in "sex," I'm typing in "gaytube," "gay porn," "gayxxx," gay whatever. I understood what Rhimes was going for, but this notion that all sex is the same and we shouldn't label any of it as being "different" for fear that we aren't being "inclusive" enough is a nice "progressive" idea that in reality serves no purpose whatsoever. What's the point in denying the color of something? For a mainstream indie, *King Cobra* has a lot of simulated *gay sex* in it and the heterosexual actors really go for it, including James Franco and Christian Slater. All the characters are gay in a narrative that's blessedly free of both ideology and gay suffering, because the suffering in *King Cobra* is caused by capitalism, and in this movie being gay isn't the point. The men in *King Cobra* have already worked through whatever issues they might have had about their sexuality, and they have other problems to deal with, and there's an actual plot that isn't about being gay—it's just a crime drama.

I suppose both *Moonlight* and *King Cobra* are "progressive" movies, insofar as they're both about things we rarely see depicted in mainstream indie films. In *Moonlight* Barry Jenkins proves, in what's only his second movie, that he has an eye for composition, texture, and rhythm, and he mostly knows what to do with the camera. I'm not totally convinced Justin Kelly's an artist yet but he can shape scenes and works well with actors and, even though the movie goes to hell in the last few minutes, he attempted something daring and new. I can't claim that *King Cobra* is a better movie than *Moonlight* but on an emotional-aesthetic level I prefer it as a gay-themed picture, because with its casual tossed-off manner it has no problem visualizing complicated reserves of gay male desire. White privilege makes it easier for these guys to connect effortlessly, and to publicly exploit their bodies and sexuality, yet very few of the sex scenes in *King Cobra* take place on porn sets, but instead are private scenes in bedrooms and living rooms that reveal the main characters' desires and motivations—

meaning that the explicit gay sex in *King Cobra* isn't dictated by its porn milieu background, and this is why the movie seems a step ahead of *Moonlight*.

Kelly gets the narrative going quickly—the story's deftly laid out—and the movie is unfussy and neutral with a dark-toned and surprisingly elegant look at times, especially given its one-million-dollar budget. If Kelly flirts with a bitchy camp aesthetic, that's mostly folded into the true crime narrative—the movie is soapy, not campy. The best scenes involve gay men talking about money, and the negotiations and power games they enact, rather than trying to illustrate how they're so shut down by society, by ideology, by homophobic parents, whatever. The most compelling scene is a long take in a sushi bar where three of the lead characters are discussing business, done in a very slow zoom and with behavioral details and funny asides and digressions that hint at the film *King Cobra* could have been, but finally it's just a soft-core exploitation movie, sleazy, energetic, and not afraid of being tacky. This occasionally reminds you that sometimes artlessness can be an aesthetic, too.

Moonlight has a 98 percent rating on Rotten Tomatoes while *King Cobra* has a 44 percent rating, and the truth lies somewhere in the middle—neither movie is as good or as bad as the critics say. *Moonlight* is a labor of love while *King Cobra* might be one but doesn't come off like it, yet I prefer *King Cobra* because this is the rare post-gay film in which no one is tortured about being gay, no one gets bullied, no one is ashamed, no one has tearfully passionate coming-out scenes, and there's no gay suffering at all—there's a murder, but it's over money. And isn't this, in our new acceptance of gay lives and equality, whether black or white, the *more* progressive view?

■ ■ ■

In the spring of 2013, men of a certain demo experienced a flicker of annoyance at how the media treated basketball player Jason Collins as some kind of baby panda who needed to be honored and praised and consoled and infantilized for his coming out on the cover of *Sports Illustrated*. Within the tyrannical homophobia of the sports world, that any man—much less a *black* one—would come out was a triumph not only for the gay community but also for pranksters everywhere, who were thrilled by the idea that what should rightly be considered a boring fact that's nobody's business was instead a shock heard briefly around the planet. This was an undeniable moment (perhaps just a footnote now) and Jason Collins was the future, though the subsequent fawning over his simple statement that he was gay still seemed in that moment like a new kind of victimization, with George Stephanopoulos interviewing him on *Good Morning America* so tenderly it was as if he was talking to a six-year-old boy. And the reign of the gay man as magical elf—who appears before us whenever he comes out as some kind of saintly, adorable ET whose sole purpose is to remind us *only* about tolerance and our prejudices, to encourage us to feel good about ourselves and to serve as a symbol instead of being just another guy—still seems in media play five years later. While watching the coverage of the 2018 Winter Olympics in PyeongChang I was constantly reminded that freestyle skier Gus Kenworthy and figure skater Adam Rippon were openly gay—a media "progressivism" that one would have assumed was by now both tone-deaf and antiquated, and yet Kenworthy and Rippon openly participated in it, encouraging an identity-politics fervor that tilted toward that same casual and mindless degradation: the Gay Man as Magical Elf.

The Gay Man as Magical Elf was such a widespread (if tricky) part of self-patronization that by now you would expect the chill members of the gay community to respond with cool indifference to the question of anybody else's gayness. Even now, however, the sweet and smiley and sexually unthreatening elf with liberal values and a positive attitude is supposed to transform everyone into noble gay-loving protectors—again, as long as the gay in question toes the party line, isn't messy or *too* sexual, negative or angry and offers no contradictions and is certainly not conservative or Christian. Sanctimonious voices in the media, straight and gay alike, tell us that all gay people should be canonized as long as they share the same uniform values—speak like this, express themselves within this range, only believe in this, only support this, vote for this. (The angry and funny and outspoken pop star Morrissey is an anomaly, calling out contradictions and hypocrisies in society yet he always seems to be chastised by the press and on social media because he's speaking honestly and doesn't buy into the accepted narrative of the Applebee's Gay.) The corporate heralding of gayness has always felt alienating to some of us: the upbeat press release, the smiling mask to assure us everything's awesome. The gay man who comes out and *doesn't* want to represent the status quo, and doesn't feel like part of a homogenized gay culture or even rejects it and refuses to be a likable role model—in other words, the disappearing rebel—seems to have gone missing in society. The gay men who made crude jokes about other gays on social media, or who expressed their hopelessness when *Modern Family* was rewarded for its depiction of a gay couple and the heterosexual playing the most simpering queen on TV won Emmys for it, they're either AWOL or severely underrepresented. Gay dudes who reject the cult of likability by remaining real and flawed simply aren't what the gatekeepers of gay culture necessarily want. But it's not what the gatekeepers of *any* culture seem to want now, either.

■ ■ ■

In April 2013 I was invited to the GLAAD (Gay and Lesbian Alliance Against Defamation) media awards by one of my agents. The agency had bought a table and she asked me to be her date. Bill Clinton was being celebrated that evening, which I immediately thought was bizarre since Clinton signed DOMA, the Defense of Marriage Act, and implemented Don't Ask, Don't Tell but then I remembered that GLAAD had also honored Brett Ratner the year after he'd (innocuously, I thought) jokingly told the moderator during a Q&A after a screening of one of his movies that "rehearsal is for fags" and was forced to repent. When I accepted the invitation I had no idea that GLAAD harbored any resentment toward me as someone who occasionally expressed his distaste for stereotypical Hollywood representations in transgressive language on his Twitter account. In fact, GLAAD had nominated *The Rules of Attraction* as movie of the year in 2003; it lost to *The Hours,* where (of course) a tormented gay man with AIDS commits suicide by throwing himself out of a window in front of Meryl Streep. In *Rules,* a cool-with-being-gay college student (played by Ian Somerhalder) falls in love with the campus drug dealer and ladies' man (James Van Der Beek) but is merely bummed out by his rejection. This should be too dumbly obvious to state—something one increasingly has to do in the current climate—but I've always supported gay rights. For anyone who's gay it's in your DNA to do so. I hadn't, however, always tolerated how gay people have been portrayed in various media and had vented my distaste for this on Twitter. Since I knew a lot of gay men agreed with me—that gay men were represented in some kind of unending gay minstrel show in movies and on TV, often created by writers and producers who were gay themselves, or else were just conveniently ignored, and not a single Best Picture nominee in 2012 had a gay character in it—I assumed that the proud liberal community I supposedly belonged to was as inclusive as I was harmlessly critical. Hey, it's a *Twitter* account, guys, *move on*. Certainly, in the spring of 2013 I hadn't fucked up as many gay lives as Bill Clinton had.

Yet the day before the event my agent texted me that GLAAD was "furious" about a couple of tweets I'd posted over the last few years, and that because of them, my invitation had been withdrawn. I was sitting in a theater with my boyfriend of four years and about to watch a matinee of *Oblivion*, starring Tom Cruise (I won't get into the layers of gay irony here) as the agent sent me part of GLAAD's email to her along with their "instructions" and saying that they hoped I wasn't "disappointed." And I was a little disappointed, at first, but after thinking it through, I can't say I was surprised, considering how literal-minded and irony-free GLAAD seemed to a lot of us. The "instructions" also requested that I wouldn't go public or tweet about their decision to disinvite me and suggested, as they often do with anyone who has somehow "transgressed" the GLAAD rules of humorless social etiquette, that I have a "sit down" with them. I could only think,

Where in the hell were we—gay elementary school? I apologized to my agent for any embarrassment this might have caused her and then started tweeting.

■ ■ ■

In the late spring of 2013, a lot of gay people supported me after I tweeted about not being allowed to go to the GLAAD awards. It made news in certain circles, yet, in my view, it was GLAAD's party and they could invite or disinvite anyone they wanted to. But, since its inception, the organization had been divisive within the community (as I myself had become, to some degree), and for all their good deeds, many considered them almost fascistically PC in confused ways: they *preached* tolerance but would quickly bitch-slap anybody who didn't fall in stride with their agenda and ideology. The fact that GLAAD relentlessly bullied Alec Baldwin after he lashed out at paparazzi with gay slurs without ever acknowledging that he'd recently played an unstereotypical gay dude in *Rock of Ages* (a film directed by a gay man) and even had kissed Russell Brand on the mouth partly explains why he has never been a "traitor" to the community I belong to. The corporate-gay overreaction to Baldwin's heated comments, namely the effort to falsely place Baldwin into a hate-speech narrative, was one of many reasons why I never wanted GLAAD to represent me in matters of cultural thought.

What GLAAD reinforces is the notion that gay men are oversensitive babies who need to be coddled and protected—not from the hideous anti-gay assaults in Russia, the Muslim world, China, or India, to name a few, but within *domestic cultural* sentiments. GLAAD was at the red-hot center for the creation of the magical elf as an absurdly high-minded and cutesy role model—hopefully a victim with great pecs—and had often applauded the stereotypes we saw paraded around in embarrassing queer movies and degrading retro sitcoms as "positive" simply because they were, um, *gay*. All the while they conveniently disregarded the truth, that a silent majority of gay men actively loathed and resisted the caricatures on display. (And no, GLAAD, they didn't hate themselves—"self-hating" being the favorite pejorative aimed at any dissenters from the corporate directive.) Activists dive-bombing other gays who had simply expressed an opinion they didn't like, or that didn't lean toward their agenda, meant that their safe space, like the rest of the culture, had begun to exist on a fairly simplistic plane. A barbed observation—even remarks—tweeted by a gay man about other gay men in Hollywood and *not* directed at anyone became, in GLAAD's new world order, hate speech.

When a community prides itself on its differences and its uniqueness and then bans people because of how they express themselves—not for acts of hate speech but simply because it doesn't like their opinions—a corporate fascism has been put into play that ought to be seriously reconsidered, not just by GLAAD but by everyone. The problem a lot of my supporters had was simple: if you're not the gay man as magical elf, you automatically run the risk of being ostracized by the elite gay community. And, anyway, what was GLAAD trying to protect by disinviting me? What statement were they making? We won't tolerate *tweets*? We won't invite someone we think is dickish? An organization holding an awards ceremony they claim represents *all* gays and yet also feeling they can choose *which* gays can and cannot be members of the party is, on the face of it, ridiculous. The takeaway also seems simple: if you aren't a happy homosexual comrade promoting what they define as acceptable values and pimping for GLAAD, you're somehow defaming the cause. But *what* cause? Likability? Capitulation? That we all must be the same? That we all need to be actors? Later that spring, an openly gay director Facebooked me and said he agreed with much of what I'd tweeted—as did plenty of gay dudes in the industry, though a few said they would have worded things differently—and he, too, was especially aggravated to see gay men portrayed in entertainment as either victims or bitchy clowns or queeny best friends, though admittedly in 2013 at that point there were a few shows that balanced things out, with the evil Republican on *Scandal* and the slobby Max Blum on the short-lived *Happy Endings*. A gay TV writer said he also agreed with my tweets but couldn't understand why I cared what middlebrow gays thought about anything.

■ ■ ■

What threw GLAAD into a massive hissy fit had to do with tweets they assumed had proved that I believed gay actors couldn't play straight roles, which was a misreading of the tweets. I only said that famously gay Matt Bomer, who is publicly married to his partner, a Hollywood publicist, seemed like a weird actor to push for the role of the very straight BDSM freako Christian Grey in the adaptation of *Fifty Shades of Grey*. I thought this because there was no way a corporate entity like Comcast-NBCUniversal was going to endanger what would become a billion-dollar franchise by selecting an actor who was easily and openly gay (an openness I wholeheartedly encourage and applaud, especially for anyone with leading-man looks working in a homophobic casting biz) and who carried any baggage that could distract from the heavy heterosexual fantasy of this particular movie. For example, in a key exchange at the very beginning Anastasia questions Christian's sexuality and provokes his insulted denials—with Bomer in the role, this would become a very meta scene.

I thought this casting—already being advocated by a vocal faction on Twitter, many of whom apparently didn't know Bomer was gay—would create a distraction by mixing up the public/private life of the actor with his role as a voracious heterosexual predator. I might have been wrong about this, I suppose, and maybe women wouldn't need to reprocess the actor playing this role in order to surrender themselves to this fantasy, though the women I talked to almost unanimously said it would have made the movie even stranger and more remote for them. As a friend of a few actors who feel they can't reveal their sexuality if they want to land certain parts, I knew that for Bomer coming out couldn't have been easy and that my tweets might have been construed as bordering on insensitive, though that's exactly what rationality and logic are now often considered in this everyone-is-a-victim culture. But on the other hand, I thought, *So fucking what?* It was simply an opinion. I wasn't in any position to hire or reject Matt Bomer. I'd simply tweeted that I *thought* in this particular role there seemed to be a problem. And I disagreed with fans of his who argued that Bomer successfully played a married and straight male stripper in Steven Soderbergh's *Magic Mike,* because I didn't remember Matt in that movie at all except for the scene in which he ogled Alex Pettyfer while saying it was okay for him to screw his wife while he watched.

Ah, but tweeting that watching *Glee* was like "stepping into a puddle of HIV" and that Chris Colfer singing "Le Jazz Hot" gave me "the hivs" also outraged them. My HIV-positive friends as well as many other gay men I knew (and know) often made gallows jokes about HIV and AIDS, which helped to lessen some of the moralistic stigma surrounding the disease, and black humor always acts as a coping mechanism. If certain Hollywood liberals got pissed-off at the HIV jokes, weren't they making HIV a moral and political concern—exactly as the right-wing once had—instead of just another one of nature's fuckups that happened to hit the gay community first and hardest? What I thought was funny about this tweet was the outrageousness of connecting the seriousness of HIV with what is essentially a dumb kids' show that can be embarrassing just because it's so lamely, well, gay. I probably should've known this would enrage the Gay Police, but I didn't tweet it *at* anyone and it seemed funny at the time (and still does). I realized, in the late spring of 2013, if a gay man—or, let's face it, a straight man—can't make an HIV joke and somehow connect it with *Glee* that perhaps we were all getting lost in the French royal court of West Hollywood and, beyond that, heading toward the corporate abyss.

■ ■ ■

Because of these tweets and a few similar comments, I've been accused of being a self-loathing gay man, and I might be a little self-loathing at times—not an unattractive quality, by the way—but it's not because I'm gay. I think life is essentially hard, an existential struggle for everyone to varying degrees, and that scalding humor and rallying against life's built-in absurdities and breaking conventions and misbehaving and encouraging whatever taboo is the most honest path on which to move through the world. Sometimes that means making fun of myself or lashing out in ways that might make dumb-asses or the merely misinformed think that I hate myself for being gay and that a gay man can't tell a joke equating AIDS with Grindr (something my boyfriend and I had used a number of times) without being scorned as self-loathing is indicative of a new fascism. The real shame isn't the jokey observations but the lockstep *reaction* to them. And an even deeper shame in all of this is the fact that most gay guys—who are every bit as hilariously filthy and raunchy and un-PC as their straight counterparts—have to somehow toe GLAAD's party line in public or else be criticized and banished. A lot of them probably feel they can't be politically incorrect or provocatively vile in the current culture simply because it doesn't represent the values of the sainted cause: enforced likability and, ultimately, conformity.

This is a revised version of gay self-victimization, which supposedly is enlightened and ennobled yet doesn't really connect with any genuine ideas about liberalism and freedom. As a writer I have to believe in free speech no matter what—that's as simple and true as it gets. On a few occasions I got slammed by young, presumably straight dudes, when I tweeted about glimpsing Alexander Skarsgård naked in a locker room in West Hollywood or that I thought Adam Driver on *Girls* was the sexiest man on television. "I didn't follow you to sign up for this gay shit," someone tweeted back, and another wondered, "Why are you such a fag?" I shrugged it off and didn't make a federal case out of it, or call the local chapter of GLAAD. I didn't even bother to block them. Because once you start choosing how people can and cannot express themselves then this opens the door to a very dark room in the corporation from which there's really no escape. Can't they in return police your thoughts, and then your feelings and then your impulses? And, finally, can they police, ultimately, your dreams?

liking

I still remember a conversation I had with a close friend in the spring of 1986, when I was a senior at Bennington College. She and I were driving into town to see a movie, listening to the radio, and once the Bangles' "Manic Monday" came on I leaned over to turn the volume up, telling my friend, who was driving, that I thought their new record *Different Light* was really good and this lead single, which had just hit number two on Billboard's Hot 100, was "impeccably put-together baroque pop"—and if that sounds like something a character in *The Rules of Attraction* might say, well, that's the book I was writing then. My friend wrinkled her nose and said the song bothered her because it seemed so dumbly girly. She cited the lyric "'cause it takes me so long just to figure out what I'm gonna wear" as an example of the path the glammed-up Bangles were now heading down and noted that a man (Prince!) had written the song. I argued that "Manic Monday" could be construed as feminist because it was about a woman who works tirelessly to support herself and her unemployed boyfriend. But my companion rolled her eyes and obviously wasn't buying this interpretation; in retrospect, I realized she considered it an act of cultural appropriation three decades before this term was ever used. She'd liked the stripped-down no-nonsense lo-fi first Bangles record, but their super-slick and commercialized new one left her cold and she didn't like how the lead singer Susanna Hoffs—now deliberately being groomed for hot-babe superstardom—had sexed herself up. (For my straight male friends, the Bangles became a go-to band for the rest of that decade *because* of Hoffs.) That the whole thing bothered her so much took me completely by surprise. We'd known each other as freshmen, and she was funny, irreverent—how could this humorless take on a Bangles song be possible? I thought *Different Light* was a huge step forward for a band I'd liked since buying their first EP in 1982, and in fact this *was* a perfect pop record, the only cassette I listened to on a book tour throughout the UK earlier that year. My memories of that tour are synched with those songs, and the drama of the title track will forever be trailing me through a snowstorm in Manchester.

What shocked me about my friend's admission—and why I remember what should've been an innocuous disagreement about a pop song—was that I finally understood that you could argue about "Manic Monday" or *Different Light* or the *new* Bangles on *aesthetic* grounds. But it never crossed my mind that a smart woman might hold these dislikes for a host of other reasons: because she rejected what the new femmy Bangles were projecting; because to her the song seemed a digression; because it confirmed something that she'd always hated about the music industry. I'll never forget her mocking Susanna Hoffs's baby-doll vocals as we drove to the theater in the rainy, deserted town: "I wish it was Sunday / 'cause that's my fun day / my I don't have to run day . . ." I'd loved these vocals on a daily basis for the three months the record had been out and couldn't believe that my friend had found within this song a troubling commentary on gender. This suddenly silenced my enthusiasm, and I blushed deeply when I grasped her irritation; I didn't agree with it, but I could see where it came from, and there was no point in defending anything. We simply had two different points of view. It also made me wonder about all the swishy pandering gay stereotypes (were they, really?) I'd had to watch and reject repeatedly throughout my adolescence and young adulthood, stereotypes that my straight friends and classmates seemed to takc for granted. What should have been a small, passing moment has instead stayed with me for decades: someone I liked was offended by something I loved. I can't listen to "Manic Monday" without being reminded of that conversation my friend and I had as we drove through the hills of Vermont, to the dilapidated theater on Main Street. But in fact I was never good at realizing what might offend someone anyway.

■ ■ ■

I've been rated and reviewed since I became a published author at the age of twenty-one, and I've grown entirely comfortable in being both liked and disliked, adored and despised. This environment feels natural to me, and I've never placed much importance on the opinions that shoot in, either pro or con. The critical reputation that emerged was based on how many reviewers liked or didn't like my books, or what they thought I represented. This is how it works—and that's cool, I guess. I was the rare author who was praised as often as he was disparaged. Unlike my peers, I wasn't politely ignored if a critic didn't like my books—he or she went after me full throttle. And I doubt any other writer of my generation received worse reviews than I did—and that's not bragging or complaining, it's just the truth. But being reviewed negatively never changed the way I wrote or the topics I wanted to explore, no matter how offended some readers were by my descriptions of violence and sex. As a Gen Xer, rejecting, or more likely *ignoring* the status quo came easily to me.

One of my generation's loudest anthems was Joan Jett's "Bad Reputation," whose chorus rang out, "I don't give a damn 'bout my reputation / I've never been afraid of any deviation." And my own reputation became a target of groupthink when my conglomerate-owned publishing house decided it didn't like the contents of a particular novel I'd been given a contract to write for them and subsequently refused to publish it on the grounds of "taste"—they were offended by it. This is a story I'll return to later, but it was a scary moment for the arts—if one that has come to seem normal: in effect, a corporation was deciding what should or shouldn't be permitted, what should or shouldn't be read, what you could say and what you weren't allowed to say. The difference between then (1990) and now is that there were loud arguments and protests about this on *both* sides of the divide: people had differing opinions yet debated them rationally, driven by passion *and* logic. The embrace of corporate censorship wasn't quite as acceptable in those days. You couldn't argue that a certain HBO show shouldn't be *written,* on the grounds of its presumed (though unproven) racism. There was no such thing, yet, as *thought* crime—now an everyday accusation. People also listened to one another, and I recall that as a time when you could be fiercely opinionated and openly questioning without being considered a troll and a hater who should get banned from the "civilized" world if your conclusions turned out to be different.

■ ■ ■

On a *South Park* episode in 2015, the character Cartman and other townspeople are enthralled by Yelp, an app that lets customers rate and review restaurants, and they remind maître d's and waiters that they will be posting judgments about their meals. These Yelpers threaten to give eateries only one star out of five if they don't grant their every wish and do exactly what they want. In turn, the restaurants feel they have no choice but to comply, and the Yelpers exploit their power by asking for free dishes and making suggestions on how to improve the lighting. The employees tolerate all this with increasing frustration and anger—at one point Yelp reviewers are even compared to ISIS—before both parties finally arrive at a truce. Unbeknownst to the Yelpers, the restaurant's revenge is to contaminate their plates with every bodily fluid imaginable (and I mean *every*). The point of this episode is that patrons are now so deluded they all think they're professional critics—as in "Everyone relies on my Yelp reviews!"—even if they have no idea what the fuck they're talking about. But in depicting the restaurant's revenge it also provides a bleak commentary on what's become known as the "reputation economy." That services today are rating us *back* raises the notion of how we present ourselves online and in social media, and how individuals can both brand *themselves* there and *get* branded. When everybody claims to be a specialist, with a voice that deserves to be heard, this actually makes each person's voice less meaningful. All we've really done is to set ourselves up—to be sold to, branded, targeted, data-mined. But this is the logical endgame of the democratization of culture and the dreaded cult of inclusivity, which insists everybody has to live under the same umbrella of rules and regulations: a mandate that dictates how all of us should express ourselves and behave.

■ ■ ■

Most people of a certain age probably noticed this when they joined their very first corporation. Facebook encouraged its users to "like" things, and because this platform is where they branded themselves on the social Web for the first time, their impulse was to follow the Facebook dictum and present an idealized portrait of themselves—or of a nicer, friendlier, duller self. And this was when the twin ideas of likability and "relatability" were born, which together began to reduce all of us, ultimately, to a neutered clockwork orange, enslaved to yet another corporate version of the status quo. To be accepted, we had to follow an upbeat morality code under which everything had to be liked and everybody's voice had to be respected, and anyone who held negative or unpopular opinions that weren't inclusive—in other words, a simple *dis*like—would be shut out of the conversation and ruthlessly shamed. Absurd doses of invective were often hurled at the supposed troll, to the point where the original "offense" or "transgression" or "insensitive dickish joke" or "idea" seemed negligible by comparison. In the new digital post-Empire age we're accustomed to rating TV shows, restaurants, video games, books, even doctors, and we mostly give positive reviews because nobody wants to look like a hater. And even if you aren't one, that's what you're labeled if you steer away from the herd.

But meanwhile, and increasingly, the corporations are also rating us (as noted above). Sharing-economy companies like Uber and Airbnb rate their customers and shun those who don't make the grade. With personal opinions and critical responses flowing in both directions, people began worrying about how they measured up. I was once briefly intrigued by the possibility that the reputation economy might stimulate the culture of shaming—of being more honest and critical than ever—but the bland corporate-culture idea of protecting yourself by "liking" everything, of being falsely positive in order to fit in with the gang, has only grown stronger and more pervasive. Everyone keeps posting positive reviews in hopes of getting the same in return. Rather than embracing the truly contradictory nature of human beings, with all of our biases and imperfections and flaws, we continue to transform ourselves into virtuous robots—or at least what *our side* thinks a virtuous robot should be. This in turn has led to the awful idea—and booming business—of reputation management, where firms are hired to help shape a more likable, relatable You. Devoted to gaming the system, this new practice is a form of deception, an attempt to erase (strangely) both subjectivity and objectivity, to evaluate through mass intuition, for a very high price.

■ ■ ■

Like virtually everything, the reputation company's only goal is to make money. It urges us to adopt the dull conformity of corporate culture and forces us to react defensively by varnishing our imperfect selves so we can sell and be sold things—because who wants to take a ride or rent a house or treat a medical condition with anybody who doesn't have a good online reputation? The new economy depends on everyone maintaining a reverentially conservative and eminently practical attitude: keep your mouth shut and your skirt long, be modest and don't have any fucking opinions except those of the majority groupthink in that moment. The reputation economy is another instance of the *blanding* of our society, even though the enforcement of groupthink in social media has only increased anxiety and paranoia, because those who eagerly approve of the reputation economy are, of course, also the most scared. What happens if they lose what has become their most—if not only—valuable asset? This is another ominous reminder of how financially desperate people are, and that the only tool they have to raise themselves up the economic ladder is their sparklingly upbeat reputation with its fake flawless surface—which only adds to their ceaseless worry, their endless need to be liked, liked, liked. What people seem to forget in this miasma of false narcissism, and in our new display culture, is that empowerment doesn't come from liking this or another, but from being true to our messy contradictory selves—which sometimes does, in fact, mean being a hater.

There are limits to showcasing your most flattering assets because, despite how genuine and authentic we might think we are, we're still just manufacturing a construct for social media, no matter how accurate it actually is or appears to be. What gets *erased* are the contradictions inherent in all of us. Those of us who reveal flaws and inconsistencies or voice unpopular ideas suddenly become terrifying to the ones caught up in a world of corporate conformity and censorship that rejects the opinionated and the contrarian, corralling everyone into harmony with somebody else's notion of an ideal. Very few people want solely to be negative or difficult, but what if those exact qualities were attached to the genuinely interesting, compelling and unusual—and couldn't there then be a real conversation? The greatest crime being perpetrated in this new world is that of stamping out passion and silencing the individual.

■ ■ ■

As I was completing *American Psycho* in the fall of 1989, I showed some pages of it to the person I'd found myself having a relationship with at the time, a lawyer on Wall Street who was a few years older than me, from Virginia, good-looking and closeted—meaning since I wasn't officially out yet we presented ourselves as simply friends, though, of course, close acquaintances knew otherwise but not necessarily the people he worked with at Milbank, Tweed, Hadley & McCloy. Since we'd been together for a year, Jim naturally was curious about what I'd been working on, and because I hadn't shown anyone a word from the book once I began writing it two years earlier, I thought it would be okay if I let him take a look. In a few minor respects he had influenced the creation of Patrick Bateman, even if it primarily was a novel that expressed my personal pain when I was struggling and failing to accept adulthood in those lost yuppie years of the late 1980s. After reading two chapters that had caught his attention, Jim turned to me—I was editing the manuscript on the other side of the bed—and said, "You're going to get into trouble." I remember very clearly my flash of panic, and also the confusion swirling around me as I turned to him, looking up from the pages I was editing, and asked, "What do you mean?" He'd just finished the section that leads into the first rape, and subsequent murder, of a woman—the lunch with Bethany and what follows afterward—and simply said, "You're going to get into trouble for that." I instantly became annoyed and dismissive because this had never crossed my mind. I'd written most of that scene more than a year and a half earlier and only recently had added the more violent details; I'd begun thinking of *American Psycho* as so stylized that it bordered on being an experimental novel, one that hardly anyone would ever read. If the book was regarded on *that* level, how could I get into trouble?

But I also realized that if Jim—a quiet, levelheaded Princeton grad who was always calm and low-key, never prone to drama—thought this might be true then it automatically carried a weight, particularly given how matter-of-factly he'd said it. I stared at him and asked, "Who am I going to get in trouble with?" And he said, "Everybody." He read out loud a few lines about a rape that devolves quickly and viciously into murder—hard-core violence, definitely, but something I felt was justified within the context of who and what I was writing about. Hearing Jim pull out those isolated lines, I supposed, *could* offend someone, though not within the narrative itself. This was an aesthetic intention of the portrait I was trying to paint—with those colors, with that brush—and I felt the explosions of violence were necessary to my vision. This was my dramatic instinct. There were no rules. "What if," I said, "it's all in his head?" "Is it?" Jim asked. "I don't know," I remember saying. "Sometimes I think it's all in his head, and then at other times I don't." Jim glanced at the pages he was holding and then looked back at me. "It doesn't matter," he said. "You're going to get into trouble anyway." While Jim's initial response didn't have any impact on the book—I changed nothing on account of it—as I finished my editing and rewriting, his reaction was always hovering somewhere in my mind, even after I turned in *American Psycho* to my publisher that December and it started moving through the usual production schedule. But as it was read and edited by my editor, then copyedited, then handed over to the book designer, the rumblings began. People at Simon & Schuster were offended. Women were especially offended, but the mixture of violence, sexuality, and the sick-joke sensibility made the book seem shockingly misogynistic to some men as well. The media started picking up on the discomfort within S&S, which was pressing on—the cover already designed and approved—toward a publication date in January, now only months away. And, just as Jim had predicted a year earlier, late one night in his loft on Bond Street, I was definitely in trouble.

■ ■ ■

The book was canceled in November 1990, two months before the release date Simon & Schuster had announced back in the spring. Bound galleys had been distributed, and some early readers defended (whether they read it or not) the book I believed I'd written—a black farce with an unreliable narrator—but this didn't matter: the noise from the offended was too loud, and I got kicked out of a corporation I hadn't even known I'd belonged to. Ultimately, I was allowed to keep the advance, and another publisher (actually more prestigious) bought the rights and published the book quickly as a trade paperback in the spring of 1991, a week after the combat phase of the Gulf War supposedly came to an end. As the years passed by and the controversy surrounding *American Psycho* faded, it finally was read in the spirit in which it had been created—as satire. And a few of its biggest supporters were women, feminists, including Fay Weldon and the filmmaker Mary Harron, who went on to adapt the novel into a stylish horror-comedy starring Christian Bale that was released nine years later—and unlike *Less Than Zero*, *all* of the dialogue and every scene came from the book. My one takeaway from this drama was that I came to understand I wasn't any good at recognizing what would or wouldn't tick people off, because art had never offended me.

Maybe this was a case of an actual "offense" against a privileged white male, though these rightly are never tied to oppression, but it's also true that I wasn't ever offended because I'd understood all works of art were a product of human imagination, created like everything else by flawed and imperfect individuals. Whether it was de Sade's brutality or Céline's anti-Semitism or Mailer's misogyny or Polanski's taste for minors, I was always able to separate the art from its creator and examine and value it (or not) on aesthetic grounds. Before the horrible blooming of "relatability"—the inclusion of everybody into the same mind-set, the supposed safety of mass opinion, the ideology that proposes everybody should be on the same page, the *better* page—I remember emphatically *not* wanting what our culture now demanded. Rather than respect and niceness, inclusion and safety, likability and decency, my goal was to be confronted by things. (The fact that I came from a "conventional" background—although in many ways it certainly wasn't—might, I suppose, have encouraged my desire to see the worst.) The litany of what I *did* want? To be challenged. To not live in the safety of my own little snow globe and be reassured by familiarity and surrounded by what made me comfortable and coddled me. To stand in other people's shoes and see how they saw the world—especially if they were outsiders and monsters and freaks who would lead me as far away as possible from whatever my comfort zone supposedly was—because I sensed I *was* that outsider, that monster, that freak. I craved being shaken. I loved ambiguity. I wanted to change my mind, about one thing and another, virtually anything. I wanted to get upset and even be damaged by art. I wanted to get wiped out by the cruelty of someone's vision of the world, whether it was Shakespeare or Scorsese, Joan Didion or Dennis Cooper. And all of this had a profound effect. It gave me empathy. It helped me realize that another world existed beyond my own, with other viewpoints and backgrounds and proclivities, and I have no doubt that this aided me in becoming an adult. It moved me away from the narcissism of childhood and into the world's mysteries—the unexplained, the taboo, the *other*—and drew me closer to a place of understanding and acceptance.

■ ■ ■

Lee Siegel, a writer and cultural critic, astutely predicted where we'd all end up in an essay defending Stanley Kubrick's enigmatic dream-film *Eyes Wide Shut*, whose mysteries were much derided by literal-minded audiences and critics upon its release:

> Much talk—some of it real, a lot of it fake—has been in the air over the last decade about empathy for the "other," for people different from us. But no one has dwelled on the essential otherness of a work of art. There is, after all, that hackneyed but profound notion of a willing suspension of disbelief. Genuine art makes you stake your credulity on the patently counterfeit. It takes you by surprise. And for art to take you by surprise, you have to put yourself in the power of another world—the work of art—and in the power of another person—the artist.
>
> Yet everything in our society, so saturated with economic imperatives, tells us not to surrender our interests even for a moment, tells us that the only forms of cultural expression we can trust are those that give us instant gratification, useful information, or a reflected image of ourselves. So we are flooded with the kind of art that deprecates attentiveness, tells us about the issues of the day, and corresponds to our own personalities.

This was written almost twenty years ago, and what Siegel worried about then could now be said to *define* our culture: the growing inability to accept any viewpoints that differ from the "morally superior" status quo. By coincidence I happened to be rereading this essay while listening to various college commencement speeches on YouTube in 2016, when it seemed more imperative than ever to advise students *not* to "Be Safe," as so many of these speakers seemed to suggest, but rather to advise them to boldly "Be *Un*safe" by refusing to live meekly within the bubble of the parenthesis.

The idea that if you can't identify with someone or something then it's not worth watching or reading or listening to is now commonplace in our society—and sometimes used as a weapon to attack somebody else: for not being more "woke" by failing to *make* something relatable; for being racist when perhaps the offender is, for instance, just an uninterested or clueless white person; or for being a sexual predator instead of, occasionally, plainly a douche, a boor, a loser. "I can't relate to it" had come to be shorthand for "I won't watch it," much as "I can't identify with it" now means "I won't read or listen to *that*." You hear this increasingly as a rallying cry, and not only from millennials, yet the idea behind it serves no progressive purpose; it marginalizes not only artists but also, ultimately, everybody on the planet. In essence, it's fascist. Here's the dead end of social media: after you've created your own bubble that reflects *only* what *you* relate to or what *you* identify with, after you've blocked and unfollowed people whose opinions and worldview you judge and disagree with, after you've created your own little utopia based on your cherished values, then a kind of demented narcissism begins to warp this pretty picture. Not being able or willing to put yourself in someone else's shoes—to view life differently from how you yourself experience it—is the first step toward being *not* empathic, and this is why so many progressive movements become as rigid and as authoritarian as the institutions they're resisting.

I saw this disconnection at work in Amy Pascal's speech to a gay group in 2014. A well-intentioned straight person, and formerly the head of Sony, she made a few excellent points about gay content and representation but then started talking about how we should get rid of every homophobic slur in film and TV as well as *every* stereotypical gay character, and I felt we were entering into a kind of Utopian weirdness that doesn't exist and probably *shouldn't.* I remember having the same odd concern in 2013 when at Comedy Central's James Franco roast, millennial comedian Aziz Ansari derided all the other comics because he felt they'd told an inordinate number of often "inappropriate" gay jokes. These jokes existed obviously because they had something to do with Franco's public persona, that of an earnest straight man turned super-gay supporter/experimenter/ dabbler (see *King Cobra,* for example, or his *Cruising* homage), and over the years many people both straight and gay had ribbed Franco and made fun of this on social media and in the entertainment press. On this occasion I recall feeling very distinctly that Ansari had managed to hijack the spirit of the roast—and he was, in fact, one of the first virtue-signaling celebrities I noticed. Were we now being too careful about "protecting" the gay baby pandas from crude sex jokes? Some of these jokes were funny, some weren't, but within the context of a fucking roast *everything* seemed permissible: loser white guy jokes, ugly white guy jokes, sexist jokes about women, racist jokes. It was heartening to see a live audience of white people and black people, as well as men and women of all ages, laughing hysterically at the insensitive, noninclusive and politically incorrect material told by comics, white and black, young and old, male and female. Their laughter was the undeniable corrective to Ansari's criticism: some shit's *just funny.*

Ansari was exploring a particular narrative—the idea that it might be better to protect a marginalized group from being the brunt of jokes—and this seemed problematic, because was it really so progressive to marginalize gays even further by *not* making fun of them, by not even *mentioning* them in a roast which by definition makes fun of whoever's being honored? But in this "inclusive" fantasy everyone has to be the same, must share the same values and outlook and sense of humor. The ascendant culture keeps proposing this again and again and again—until when? A genuinely inclusive idea of comedy would allow gay dudes to make fun of other gays and whoever else they wanted to, and straight people to make fun of gays or anybody else. If gay jokes are taken out of the equation, what goes next? And there's the slippery slope, the maze that no one emerges from, the dark room whose door is quickly closing behind you. Do gay guys really *need* a straight guy like Ansari to be their defender? And what was Ansari defending *at a roast*? Is there now a revised rule book for comedy and freedom of expression? Should all ideas and opinions and content and language now be *policed*? Sometimes the funniest, most dangerous comedy does not reassure you that everything's going to be okay. Exclusion and marginalization are often what *makes* a joke funny. Sometimes one's identity *is* the punch line. Laugh at everything, or you'll end up laughing at nothing. As a young writer in Ireland, James Joyce realized, "I have come to the conclusion that I cannot write without offending people."

■ ■ ■

In February 2014 I gave an interview to *Vice* (UK) to help promote *The Canyons*, a film I'd written and helped finance. There was still the hopeful idea that if Paul Schrader, the director, and I talked about the movie it might somehow find an audience that would be interested in it. But there was no telling who these people might be, because *The Canyons* was an experimental, guerrilla, DIY affair that had cost $250,000 to shoot ($90,000 out of our own pockets, the rest of it crowd-funded) over twenty days in LA during the summer of 2012, and which starred controversial millennials Lindsay Lohan and porn star James Deen. The young *Vice* journalist asked me what was preoccupying me at the moment: Martin Scorsese's *The Wolf of Wall Street*, the best film I'd seen the year before; a movie I was writing for Kanye West (that never happened); my creeping misgivings about Terrence Malick; a miniseries I was developing about the Manson murders for Fox (which got canceled after another Manson series went into production at NBC); the *Bret Easton Ellis Podcast*, which I'd started a few months earlier; a new novel I was contemplating after that disastrous week in Palm Springs with my mad friend a year earlier.

We talked about my problems with David Foster Wallace; my love of Joan Didion; my theories regarding Empire versus the post-Empire moment, which I'd delineated in a controversial article in *The Daily Beast* that Tina Brown had published in 2011. And we talked, of course, about the doomed theatrical release of *The Canyons*. But the first question the young journalist asked me wasn't about the movie but why I was always referring to millennials as Generation Wuss on my Twitter feed and podcast. And I answered her honestly, unprepared for the level of noise my comments would raise in the UK, and beyond, once the *Vice* piece was posted.

As it happens, by then I'd been living with a millennial for almost five years (twenty-two years my junior), and I was alternately charmed and exasperated by how he and his friends—as well as other millennials I'd met and interacted with both in person and on social media—lived their lives. I had been occasionally tweeting about my amusement and frustration under the banner "Generation Wuss" in recent years. My huge generalities touched on millennials' oversensitivity, their sense of entitlement, their insistence that they were always right despite sometimes overwhelming proof to the contrary, their failure to consider anything within its context, their joint tendencies of overreaction and passive-aggressive positivity—incidentally, all of these misdemeanors happening only sometimes, not always, and possibly exacerbated by the meds many this age had been fed since childhood by overprotective, helicopter moms and dads mapping their every move. These parents, whether tail-end baby boomers or Gen Xers, now seemed to be rebelling against their own rebelliousness because they felt they'd never really been loved by their own selfish narcissistic true-boomer parents, and who as a result were smothering their kids and not teaching them how to deal with life's hardships about how things actually work: people might not like you, this person will not love you back, kids are really cruel, work sucks, it's hard to be good at something, your days will be made up of failure and disappointment, you're not talented, people suffer, people grow old, people die. And the response from Generation Wuss was to collapse into sentimentality and create victim narratives, instead of grappling with the cold realities by struggling and processing them and then moving on, better prepared to navigate an often hostile or indifferent world that doesn't care if you exist.

■ ■ ■

I never pretended to be an expert on millennials and my harmless tweeting was based solely on personal observation. The reactions to the tweets ran, predictably, along generational lines. One of the worst arguments my partner and I endured happened when we first started living together in 2010, and it revolved around the Tyler Clementi suicide in New Jersey earlier that year. Clementi was an eighteen-year-old Rutgers student who killed himself because he *felt* he'd been bullied by his roommate. Dharun Ravi hadn't ever touched or threatened Tyler, but had—unbeknownst to Tyler—used a webcam on his dorm-room computer to film him making out with another man, and then tweeted about it. Deeply embarrassed by this prank, Tyler threw himself off the George Washington Bridge a few days later. The fight I had with my millennial partner was about cyberbullying and imagined versus genuine hands-on threats and actual assault of any kind. Was this just the case of an overly sensitive Generation Wuss "snowflake" (I enjoyed using this term because it seemed, amazingly, to press so many buttons) and had this tragic death made the national news because of how trendy the idea of cyberbullying had become? Or had a terribly sensitive young man simply snapped because he'd been brought down by his own shame and was subsequently turned into a victim/hero (they're the same thing now for millennials) by a media eager to dispense with context—and turn Ravi into a monster just because he'd played a pretty harmless freshman dorm-room prank? People my own age tended to agree with my tweets referencing the case, but those my boyfriend's age were prone to disagree vehemently.

Then again, my reaction had something to do with the fact that I was looking at millennials from the POV of a generation as pessimistic and ironic as any other that ever roamed the earth. Depending on what chart you're consulting I was one of the very first members of Generation X, so when I heard about millennials being so damaged by cyberbullying that it became a gateway to suicide, it was, admittedly, difficult for me to process—was this a joke? Yet even my boyfriend agreed that Generation Wuss was far too sensitive, especially when facing any criticism, and he said he'd often noticed this in chats and threads, on Reddit, Twitter, Facebook. Unlike any previous generation, they had so many outlets to display whatever they wanted (thoughts, feelings, art) that it often went—unfettered, unedited—instantly and globally everywhere, and because of this freedom (or lack of any restraints at all) a lot of the time it tended to seem rushed and kind of shitty, but that was okay. It's just the nature of things now, for everybody. (*The Canyons* felt like that to many people.) Yet when millennials were *criticized* for this sort of content, or for anything, really, they seemed to get so defensive they either collapsed into a spiraling depression or lashed out at the critical parties and called them haters, contrarians, trolls. This forced you to look again at the people who raised them, coddling them with praise and trying to shield them from the grim sides of life, which might well have created children who, as adults, *appeared* highly confident, competent and positive but at the hint of darkness or negativity often became paralyzed and unable to react except with disbelief and tears—*You just victimized me!*—and retreated, in effect, into their childhood bubbles.

■ ■ ■

My generation was raised in a fantasy world at the height of the Empire: our baby boomer parents were the most privileged and best-educated children of the (so-called) Greatest Generation and enjoyed the economic prosperity of postwar America. While coming of age in the second and third stages of this era, people like me realized in the 1970s and 1980s that all this was by now, like most fantasies, more or less a lie. So we rebelled with irony and negativity, both numbness and attitude, or else just conveniently checked out, since we had enough money to do so. Compared to millennial reality, ours wasn't one of economic uncertainty and hardship; we had the luxury to be depressed and ironic and cool and solvent all at once. Anxiety and neediness became the defining aspects of Generation Wuss, and when the world didn't offer any financial cushion then you had to rely on your social media presence: maintaining it, keeping the brand in play, striving to be liked, to be liked, to be liked, an actor. And this created a further and ceaseless anxiety, which was why if people were snarky about this generation they were simply written off as a dick—case closed. No negativity allowed: we're only asking to be admired in the display culture we were raised in. But this excuse is problematic because it limits debate. If we're all silenced into liking everything—the millennial dream—won't we instead be having (boring) conversations about how great it all is, and how often you've been liked on Instagram? In the spring of 2014 their iconic site BuzzFeed announced it would no longer run anything construed as "negative"—and if this notion keeps spreading, what will ultimately happen to discourse and debate? Will it cease to exist? If there doesn't seem to be any *economic* path toward improving your circumstances, then the currency of popularity becomes the norm and also why you want to have thousands of people liking you on Twitter, Facebook, Instagram, Tumblr, wherever—and why, like an actor, you'll try *desperately* to be liked. Your only hope of elevating yourself in society is through your brand, your profile, your status on social media. A friend of mine—in his early twenties—remarked recently that millennials are more curators than artists, a tribe of "aestheticists." Any young artist who goes on Tumblr, he told me, doesn't actually want to *create* art—only to steal the art or *be* the art.

■ ■ ■

I'd forgotten about the *Vice* interview until the "Generation Wuss" component caused a minor explosion in the press. I was immediately asked to appear on talk shows and podcasts and radio programs to discuss "this phenomenon." Though, as noted above, those who agreed with my tossed-off assessments skewed older, I was surprised by the number of young people who followed along as well, chiefly millennials with complaints about their peers. The older fringe wanted to share examples, which ran along the lines of a father watching in frustration as his son participated in a tug-of-war game with his classmates on the field of his elementary school, only to be stopped after a minute or two by the kindly coach, who announced the game was officially a tie, told the kids they all did a great job, and gave everyone a ribbon. But occasionally guilt-ridden parents told darker stories, chastising themselves for coddling kids who, when finally faced with middle- or high-school traumas, drifted into drugs as an escape . . . into *actual* trauma. Parents kept begging me to understand how tormented they were by the oppressive insistence to reward their kids constantly, no matter what, and that in doing so they effectively debilitated them from coping with the failures we all confront as we get older, leaving their children unequipped to deal with inevitable pain.

I didn't accept any of the TV, radio or online invitations in the spring of 2014 because I hadn't actually studied millennials or any other "generations" that seemed to be arriving behind them: Generation Z, the Founders, whoever. I never wanted to be the old geezer complaining about the next wave of offspring who were supplanting his own, though certain people definitely thought that's exactly who I was. As someone who'd satirized my generation for their materialism, and shallowness, and passivity that *Less Than Zero* bordered on, and then crossed over into, amorality, I didn't think pointing out aspects that I'd noticed in millennials was a big deal. But because of how our 24/7 news cycle runs itself dry and elevates certain voices who shouldn't necessarily be heard, I *was* briefly considered an "expert" and bombarded with emails and tweets. What the *Vice* interviewer didn't allow was that as someone who was *living* with a millennial I'd be sympathetic or, at most, harmlessly critical.

I never forgot the hellish year when my college-educated boyfriend looked for a job and could find only nonpaying internships, while also having to contend with a demeaning sexual atmosphere that places such a relentlessly superficial emphasis on looks (Tinder being, as of 2018, the most prevalent example) that it made the way *my* generation hooked up seem positively chaste and innocent by comparison. So I was sympathetic to their neurosis, narcissism and foolishness, to their having been raised in the aftermath of 9/11, born into two wars, a brutal recession, endless school shootings and the election of a president they couldn't tolerate. It wasn't hard to be sympathetic. But maybe I was more like Lena Dunham on her TV series *Girls*, which examined her own generation with a caustic, withering eye yet also remained supportive. And this is crucial: you can be both. In order to be an artist, to raise yourself above the overreacting fear-based din in which criticism is considered elitist, you *need* to be both. This, however, hasn't been easy to do because millennials don't seem capable of accepting this kind of cold-eyed, realistic and sometimes fallow take on themselves. And it's why Generation Wuss only pleads now, *Please, please, please, only give positive feedback, please . . .*

■ ■ ■

A cultural low point of 2015 was the effort by at least two hundred members of PEN America, a leading literary organization to which most writers belong, to *not* present the survivors of the *Charlie Hebdo* massacre in Paris with a newly established Freedom of Expression Courage Award. Not everyone admires this satirical weekly magazine's lewd cartoons and takedowns of Catholicism, Judaism and Islam (these including obscene drawings of Muhammad), but some people really like it, others are offended by it, and before the massacre it hadn't even been selling all that well. When two *offended* Islamist gunmen burst into *Charlie Hebdo*'s offices that January and murdered twelve staff members while shouting "God is great!" and "The prophet is avenged!" people everywhere were shocked but perhaps not surprised—this was where we had been for a while.

And it seemed appropriate for PEN to acknowledge this loss by giving *Charlie Hebdo* a Freedom of Expression award in May at their annual gala in New York. And yet, there were a few American writers who nuanced this tragedy into a sentimental narrative about the case and encouraged boycotting this recognition of it. Their argument was that *Charlie Hebdo* made fun of people who were already marginalized, and by granting this award PEN would be "valorizing selectively offensive material: material that intensifies the anti-Islamic, anti-Maghreb, anti-Arab sentiments already prevalent in the Western world." My reaction was the same one I'd had to similar *sentiments* that were being voiced over the past few years, except now swifter and harder: So. Fucking. What. Should any murder be rationalized away because somebody got offended by how an opinion was expressed?

The writers who were boycotting the PEN award had decided to draw a line where freedom of speech should start and where it should end—and once again I began imagining the frightening muzzle that increasingly proposed itself to me, in which one faction of our society demands the censorship of another faction in the name of their own ideas of noble intentions and notions of peace and goodwill. I never assumed that PEN was honoring any specific *content*, but rather that it was honoring a *principle*. The award was ultimately given to *Charlie Hebdo*, because many more PEN members believed the magazine deserved the award. But there were still the two hundred who were *offended* and felt *Charlie Hebdo* went "too far" in its satire, which suggested there was a *limited* number of targets that humorists and satirists were *allowed* to pursue. These protesters were mostly Americans. So, where were *we* coming from?

■ ■ ■

If you're a smart white person who happens to be so traumatized by something that you refer to yourself in conversation as a "survivor-victim," you probably should contact the National Center for Victims and ask them for help. If you're a Caucasian adult who can't read Shakespeare or Melville or Toni Morrison because it might trigger something harmful and such texts could damage your hope to define yourself through your victimization, then you need to see a doctor, get into immersion therapy or take some meds. If you feel you're experiencing "micro-aggressions" when someone asks you where you are from or "Can you help me with my math?" or offers a "God bless you" after you sneeze, or a drunken guy tries to grope you at a Christmas party, or some douche purposefully brushes against you at a valet stand in order to cop a feel, or someone merely insulted you, or the candidate you voted for wasn't elected, or someone correctly identifies you by your gender, and you consider this a massive societal dis, and it's triggering you and you need a safe space, then you need to seek professional help. If you're afflicted by these traumas that occurred *years* ago, and that is still a part of *you* years later, then you probably are still sick and in need of treatment. But victimizing oneself is like a drug—it feels so delicious, you get so much attention from people, it *does* in fact define you, making you feel alive and even *important* while showing off your supposed wounds, no matter how minor, so people can lick them. Don't they taste so *good*?

This widespread epidemic of self-victimization—defining yourself in essence by way of a *bad* thing, a trauma that happened in the past that you've let *define* you—is actually an illness. It's something one needs to resolve in order to participate in society, because otherwise one's not only harming oneself but also seriously annoying family and friends, neighbors and strangers who *haven't* victimized themselves. The fact that one can't listen to a joke or view specific imagery (a painting or even a tweet) and that one might characterize everything as either sexist or racist (whether or not it legitimately is) and therefore harmful and intolerable—ergo nobody else should be able to hear it or view it or tolerate it, either—is a new kind of mania, a psychosis that the culture has been coddling. This delusion encourages people to think that life should be a smooth utopia designed and built for their fragile and exacting sensibilities and in essence encourages them to remain a child forever, living within a fairy tale of good intentions. It's impossible for a child or an adolescent to move past certain traumas and pain, though not necessarily for an adult. Pain can be useful because it can motivate you and it often provides the building blocks for great writing and music and art. But it seems people no longer want to learn from past traumas by navigating through them and examining them in their context, by striving to understand them, break them down, put them to rest and move on. To do this can be complicated and takes a lot of effort, but you would think someone in that much pain would try to figure out how to lessen it, however great the cost, instead of flinging it at others expecting them to automatically sympathize with you and not recoil with irritation and disgust.

■ ■ ■

In the summer of 2016 the University of Chicago sent a letter to its incoming class of 2020 stating in essence that no "trigger warnings" or "safe spaces" would be allowed on campus, that there would be no crackdown on micro-aggressions and that visiting speakers would be allowed to speak without being boycotted because a fraction of the student body felt they'd be victimized—all of which had been almost ubiquitous at campuses around the country that year. The announcement was greeted by almost everyone with a huge sigh of exhausted relief; this seemed to mark a forward movement, a progression. Instead of coddling, babying, and letting students victimize themselves, here was the notion of helping these students become adults by forcing them to confront a world that's often hostile to individual dreams and ideals and restoring the university as a place where young adults might, instead of shutting discussions down, build themselves up by encountering ideas that differed from their own, ideas that could lead them beyond the narcissism of childhood and adolescence and enable them to absorb multiple views on any given issue—*both* sides of an opinion, a thought, an idea—that is, to expand their horizons, not narrow them. As a vital part of becoming an adult, questioning the status quo about *anything* should be encouraged. But clamping your hands over your ears and stomping your feet and demanding safe spaces and abhorring contrary ideas for fear of being victimized finally seemed to be held in check for once, at least at this one institution. Disgust with this victim culture, which exploded during the Obama era, also proved to be an ominous factor later that year with the election of Donald Trump. And one couldn't help but wonder if this surprising result might not also have been a *rejection* of the party-line mentality, another form of *resistance*.

■ ■ ■

Post-election, and well into 2017, a few of my friends and acquaintances, as well as my millennial partner of eight years, were undergoing a hangover psychosis, with no end in sight. The building that had been inhabited by liberal identity-obsessed elitists was now, after eight years of an Obama hep-cat style and sensibility, being deconstructed—in fact, decimated—by disruptors who'd taken over and were playing by an entirely new set of rules. Not only that, but these disruptors were telling those confused by their new rules to go fuck themselves—and rightly so; they won the election, it was their turn. But people were *still* fighting the fact that this man had been elected, fairly and legally, and was now actually residing in the White House, and yet they were constantly gasping, at every turn, "That's *so* not presidential." It was as if they still didn't recognize what we'd all seen throughout the campaign when the disruptor played with that rule book and blew up perceived truths about what *was* presidential, how campaigns should be run, how social media could be used to create supporters. This game plan is what ultimately made the media look like an old-school anachronism unable to comprehend either the playbook or the electoral mood, instead flailing around and wasting everybody's time by hectoring about what Trump did and said *literally*, while these anarchists in the shadows just smiled to themselves in triumph. Liberalism used to concern itself with freedoms I'd aligned myself with, but during the 2016 campaigns, it finally hardened into a warped authoritarian moral superiority movement that I didn't want to have anything to do with.

Meanwhile, people had branded themselves, somewhat touchingly, as the Resistance. But what were they resisting and what were we supposed to do about it? Posters all around my neighborhood in West Hollywood urged me to resist, resist, resist—most prominently on the gates in front of LA's most famous gay bar, the Abbey, on the corner of Robertson and Santa Monica Boulevard. Some of us who *hadn't* voted for Trump, and who decades ago had precisely identified what he might be capable of (see *American Psycho*) were wondering what exactly the targets might be. And who was telling us to resist, um, whatever? Certainly not people who'd voted for the losing candidate? We were supposed to be listening to them? Was this just an elaborate joke, an art project, a hoax? What were we supposed to be resisting? During the winter of 2016 and into 2017 I myself began to resist the meltdowns I'd been witnessing at dinners and on social media and late-night TV, and too many times in my own home, in the aftermath of Trump's victory. I found myself resisting, too, the hysterical wails about this unfair disruption of the status quo, aka the Establishment, which itself decried the dismantling of the political narrative we'd all grown accustomed to and that had eagerly expected the Obama era to effortlessly resume with another Clinton in the White House. (This had alarmed me during the campaign, suggesting as it did a movement backward instead of forward, regardless of this Clinton's gender.) When this didn't happen, well, it was just too much for some people to accept. This wasn't the usual disappointment about election results—this was fear and horror and outrage that it seemed would never subside and not just for members of Generation Wuss, like my partner, but also for real grown-ups in their forties and fifties and sixties, so unhinged that their team hadn't won they began using words like "apocalypse" and "Hitlerian." Sometimes, when listening to friends of mine, I'd stare at them while a tiny voice in the back of my head started sighing, *You are the biggest fucking baby I've ever fucking heard in my entire fucking life and please you've got to fucking calm the fuck down—I get it, I get it, you don't like fucking Trump but for fuck's sake enough already for fuck's sake.*

■ ■ ■

Just as I soon began tuning out anyone who shrilly insisted Trump had called all Mexicans "rapists" (only once, in the speech announcing his campaign, an example of how unpolished he was and what ultimately drew voters to him) I also began to tune out those who relentlessly stated that Hillary Clinton had won the popular vote (yes, basically in New York and California) and these various statements and mantras started reminding me—as the resistance continued—of the complaints of spoiled children at a birthday party when they didn't win the relay race, and who wanted the race rerun with different rules, while stomping their feet, arms crossed, pinched faces crimson and wet with tears. The legions of the disappointed had failed to get over the outcome of the election, failed to move on, and at times it became appalling, almost unbearable, that there were no signs of accepting one of life's simple if brutal truths: you win some, you lose some. "You Can't Always Get What You Want" was the background music of the Trump campaign, a boomer elegy about '60s optimism sliding into disillusionment and finally a resigned pragmatism, and it was played at all of Trump's rallies as well as after his victory speech, sealing the deal. In these contexts it always sounded mysterious:

mournful and rousing, ironic and playful, fraught with multiple meanings, and it had an eerie, teasing quality.

The childlike disbelief had manifested itself immediately after the election in embarrassing ways, from morning-after posts titled "What Am I Going to Tell My Daughter?" (one friend suggested telling her Trump won, that shit happens, grow up, this is how the world works—and next time find a better candidate) to teachers at a private school where a few of my friends sent their children denouncing the bad new president in their classrooms, which caused one parent who'd supported Trump to ask the principal how such attitudinizing could be justified in front of her *five-year-old* child—from a teacher who was an *adult*, no less. There seemed to be no point in even addressing the pink pussy hats and women walking around dressed as giant vaginas in protest, or Ashley Judd performing some slam poetry about her menstrual cycle and Madonna announcing that she wanted to blow up the White House.

■ ■ ■

In the week after the election, I had a few random dinners with male friends who'd voted for Hillary. I hadn't voted for anyone, not only because I lived in rest-assured California but also because during the campaign I'd realized I wasn't a conservative or a liberal, a Democrat or a Republican, and that I didn't buy into what either party was selling. (I'd also thought Bernie Sanders's platform was impractical to the point of absurdity.) Sometime during that year and a half I had come to understand that

I was many different things and none of them fit neatly under the ideology of one party; I disagreed with much of what both candidates said, and sometimes agreed with one or the other, but I was never convinced or swayed by either of them. And since I hadn't voted, I had no right to complain about the outcome, and I didn't. However, the friends I had dinner with that November, with whom I'd never talked politics during either the Bush or the Obama administrations, admitted how unmoored they were by this outcome. They seemed surprisingly calm, or maybe just dazed, as they confessed their shock and disappointment on election night, and then described the hangovers, literal and metaphorical, they'd endured on the morning after.

During those dinners I had that week after the election, two men had expressed their surprise and dismay that they apparently had been living in a bubble. *Living . . . in . . . a . . . bubble.* I, for some reason, hadn't been living in a bubble and knew almost as many people who'd announced their intention to vote for Trump as those who said they were voting for Hillary. It was pretty evenly split in the world I moved through—maybe 55 percent for her, 45 for him—and this might have been why the outcome hadn't seemed as shocking to me as it was to those residing in that bubble. And yet one of these men, a writer I'd known for twenty years, became even *more* hysterical as the Trump administration revealed itself, and his initial resignation turned into something desperate and childish—complete with a certainty he carried with him at another dinner, late in the summer of 2017, that Donald Trump would be impeached by September. He was sputtering, furious; everything was just a total shitshow. I stared at him in the restaurant not saying anything as that voice began sighing in my head again.

■ ■ ■

My moral ambivalence about politics in general has always left me the neutral guest at many tables. As a writer I found myself more interested in understanding my friends' thoughts and feelings than in debating the accuracy of their political forecasts or who should have won the Electoral College, or if it should even exist. I preferred, as always, to talk with them about movies and books and music and TV shows. A romantic by comparison, I'd never been a true believer that politics can solve the dark heart of humanity's problems and the lawlessness of our sexuality, or that a bureaucratic band aid is going to heal the deep contradictory rifts and the cruelty, the passion and the fraudulence that factor into what it means to be human. When my traumatized boyfriend criticized me for not being angrier about the election (five months after it happened) I shot back that I didn't want to talk about Trump anymore. I didn't care. He was elected president. Get over it. The Russians didn't destroy the Democratic Party or cause it to lose more than a thousand legislative seats in the four years leading up to the 2016 election—the Democrats did that to themselves. My boyfriend shot right back that I was being a Trump apologist, and that by simply accepting the election's results I was "colluding" with the new administration and, by extension, with Moscow.

But conspiracies were everywhere. Trump was going down. In the fall of 2017 I sat in the Polo Lounge with a well-known writer from New York who was staying at the Beverly Hills Hotel, and over dinner he informed me that he had heard "very reliably" from a "CIA operative" that a videotape of Trump urinating on two fourteen-year-old Russian prostitutes actually *did* exist, then sat back in the booth, satisfied, as if he'd laid out a fact that was guaranteed to shock me. I could tell from his expression that he thought this proved some desperate truth, but I told him that this had always sounded like a bogus rumor to me. Why hadn't the tape been released to derail Trump before the election? My friend answered with a continuation of the conspiracy theory: the Russians were using the "pee tape" as blackmail so Trump would do whatever "they" had elected him to do. I sat there silently, staring at him, and immediately ordered a third martini, one more than I usually drink.

■ ■ ■

On election night, my boyfriend relapsed into a mild opiate addiction that we thought he'd beaten over the summer. It had flared back up when Trump won the primaries but faded with the optimistic certainty of Hillary Clinton's victory. His trajectory was typical: then thirty, he was a lifetime Democrat from an upper-middle-class Jewish-showbiz family and raised in Calabasas, so his leanings were obvious, yet like so many millennials he was briefly sidetracked by Bernie Sanders and his utopian pseudo-socialism and later was disillusioned with the Democratic National Committee when Hillary won the nomination over Sanders, even though this was so inevitable that I was surprised by the outrage that coursed through many young people I knew. For about a week he'd briefly flirted with the notion of Trump because he seemed to have more in common with Sanders than Clinton did, and also because he was upset by the DEA's decision to ban a natural and organic opiate powder called kratom available in head shops everywhere that he and his friends enjoyed, so now they were disgusted by government interference and bureaucracy. But the Trump ethos repulsed him, and he took such dramatic offense against the man that I thought it bordered on derangement. I myself had long thought it was Trump's aesthetic—the needy vulgarian bully with crazy hair and orange skin—that fueled his detractors more than whatever his actual ideology might or might not be, given that he was formerly a liberal New York Democrat.

But what was happening to the person I'd been living with for almost seven years reflected the epidemic of moral superiority that was also engulfing and destroying a faction on the Left. During the months after the election I could count the number of times my inconsolable boyfriend had left the condo—and didn't need more than two hands to tally them up. His hair became long and tousled, he hadn't shaved for months, and he also developed three nonopiate addictions: Russian conspiracies as discussed on Reddit, Rachel Maddow detailing Russian conspiracy theories on MSNBC, and playing *Final Fantasy XV*. If I made even an offhand quip disparaging legacy media or fake news or the striking shifts in tone and bias that had occurred in certain national news organizations, his hackles would rise and he'd glare at me, believing deeply that *anything* the Trump administration said about fake news and the awful media could not be trusted. He was part of the supposed resistance—though too tired and stoned to actually go out and resist. The election had turned him into a wreck. At times he resembled a bedraggled and enraged Russian peasant, ranting and stomping around the condo, MSNBC blaring, yelling "Piece of shit!" whenever Trump's visage appeared on the TV screen in the living room. If he read something in any of his feeds that implicated Trump in some Russian involvement he'd jump up and down and start clapping his hands in delight. "Impeachment! Impeachment's coming. I can't fucking wait." In the early spring of 2017, this was sometimes amusing, and I would laugh, but as the year rushed forward I occasionally found myself wondering, *What have I signed on for?*

■ ■ ■

Everything had been calm prior to this seemingly endless campaign. The millennial and I never discussed politics previously, mostly because I wasn't interested and Obama was keeping him happy. We'd met during the second year of that administration, and the 2012 election barely registered on us—too preoccupied with our separate lives. Obama won, life moved on, there were no protests in the streets and the media mostly fawned, if you didn't watch Fox. But in the summer of 2015 something began to distract me, something odd was happening, something didn't seem right: the mainstream news that I had read and mostly trusted my entire adult life, legacy institutions like *The New York Times* and CNN, wasn't tracking what seemed to me a shifting reality. The disparity between what I saw happening on the ground—through social media and other news sites and simply with my own eyes and ears—and what mainstream organizations were reporting became glaringly obvious in a way that it never had before. Suddenly I began paying attention to a presidential campaign, which was—

historically—something I'd never done. And this was because of how the media had chosen to cover Donald Trump, with an absolute cluelessness. A prankster had appeared—an actual disruptor—and the press was flummoxed. The disruptor followed no rules, there was no protocol, he wasn't a politician, he didn't give a shit. He was like the Joker in *The Dark Knight:* what made him so frightening to some was that he (apparently, at least) didn't need or want anyone else's money. He insulted everyone, and his most potent insults were hurled at white, male, Establishment figures—not just Muslims, women and Mexicans. The Trump insult machine was aimed at *everybody* he had issues with, and white men got it first and far worse than anybody else, yet as the national press corps explained it, this was not the case. Trump was the poster-boy antithesis of the proud moral superiority of the Left as defined forever by Clinton's "basket of deplorables" comment, as well as by Michelle Obama's breathlessly condescending "when *they* go low, *we* go high," both of which were quoted approvingly in the legacy media.

At some point I found it distracting to be living in a country whose press had become so biased and highly corporate. Instead of trying to figure out and dismantle Trump intellectually, by changing their old-ass game plan and institutional worldview—which to battle the disruptor was what you needed to do, and learn to play by his rules—it seemed they preferred to hang on to a journalistic status quo that offered an outmoded consideration of a brand-new world that was flowering before their very eyes. Because of this, the media became so completely freaked out that they abandoned the hallmarks of neutrality and perspective. In a CNN interview in the summer of 2015, Trump said that Fox anchor Megyn Kelly was bleeding from her "eyes" and "wherever" when she aggressively questioned him during a presidential debate, and *The New York Times* decided to make this the top front-page headline the following day—the most important news of the day was supposedly how gross and juvenile Trump was in making a reference to Megyn Kelly's menstrual blood. I stared at this headline for a long time that morning, asking myself, *Why the hell is* that *the headline?* The media continued to demonstrate an inability, or unwillingness, to put themselves in the other side's shoes—their view remained fairly narrow—and I believe that if they'd reported about Trump more objectively he wouldn't have won. But if you went to *The New York Times* website you were told at one point he only had a 2.5 percent chance of winning—and this on *election eve* no less, and surely it summarized everything the *Times* had gleaned about America and its voters over the course of their extensive coverage. For me political conversations increasingly became less about policy or the candidates themselves than about how all of this was being *covered,* and to some people it seemed I was defending Trump instead of criticizing the media.

■ ■ ■

That I had little or no interest in Hillary Clinton didn't seem to bother anyone I talked to throughout 2016, when or even if the subject came up. I rarely met anyone, at least not in metropolitan Los Angeles, who had a hard-core enthusiasm for her, while during that spring and summer I encountered many people who harbored exactly that for either Donald Trump or Bernie Sanders. The majority of the millennials I was working with on a web series in the summer of 2016 shared my uninterest in Clinton, yet that didn't prevent them from going along with the media's demonization of Trump. In fact the media's panic was the root of this problem. That sense of moral superiority manifested itself when it gasped and clutched its pearls at *every* Trump outburst and joke—when taking him literally was the biggest mistake you could make as a reporter; taking Trump *literally* was about as useful as complaining about the Kardashians. There were possibly more than shadows of misogyny and sexism in how Clinton was portrayed, but she clearly had been anointed the moral savior of the Establishment, the Corporation. And when her supporters mindlessly touted her as the "most qualified candidate in history" my blood froze with dread, knowing that there was a real hunger out there for the absolute opposite: someone who might not be "qualified" at all. "Most qualified" became for many a terrifying reminder of something vague, sinister and bureaucratic that needed to be zoned out in Washington. You couldn't get around the fact that the way the legacy media was covering the election of 2016—Clinton as heroine, Trump as villain—would prove to be an utter moral disaster for the country because it helped turn Donald Trump into the biggest underdog in American political history.

■ ■ ■

I'd made Donald Trump the hero of Patrick Bateman in *American Psycho* and researched more than a few of his odious business practices, his casually brazen lying, how he'd let Roy Cohn serve as his mentor, the whiffs of racism that wouldn't necessarily be out of place in a man of his age and demographic. I'd read *The Art of the Deal* and followed his trajectory and done enough homework to make Trump a character who could float through the novel and be the person Bateman's always referencing and quoting and aspiring to be. The young men, Wall Street guys, I hung out with as part of my initial research were enthralled by him. Trump was an inspirational figure, which troubled me in 1987 and 1988 and 1989, and also why he's mentioned more than forty times in the novel. He's who Bateman is obsessed with, the daddy he never had, the man he wants to be. Maybe this was why I felt prepared when the country elected Trump as president; I once had known so many people who liked him, and I still did. One could certainly dislike the fact that he'd *been* elected and yet still understand and grasp *why* he was elected without having an absolute mental and emotional collapse. Whenever I heard certain people losing their shit about Trump my first reaction was always, *You need to be sedated, you need to see a shrink, you need to stop letting the "bad man" help you in the process of victimizing your whole life.* Why would they do that to themselves? Surely there were people—DACA recipients, or the targets of ICE raids—who had a right to freak out, but the white, upper middle class in colleges, in Hollywood, in the media, and in Silicon Valley? If you hated Trump, why would you let him win figuratively as well as literally? But that was exactly what continued to happen throughout the following year and into 2018: people who hated Trump were in fact getting Trumped. The rich and entitled liberals I knew always had the hardest time and were always the most hysterical.

■ ■ ■

In March 2017 I had dinner with two friends who were visiting LA from New York. One was a commercial director, a Jewish liberal (and I point this out because my two longest relationships were with Jewish liberal men and obviously I have a thing for them) who'd voted for Clinton but basically considered himself an independent: he had accepted the election results and moved on. My other friend, a woman in her fifties, Jewish and liberal as well, had not, and I was shocked by how frazzled she seemed. In a restaurant on Beverly Boulevard in West Hollywood, the director and I talked about the recent Oscar telecast and agreed that *La La Land* should've won Best Picture over *Moonlight*, and would have in a different world. If the transition in Washington, starting with the inauguration and leading into the spring, hadn't been depicted as *such* a disaster by the media during the Oscars' voting period, if the fear and hatred of Trump hadn't been at such a delirious fever pitch in Hollywood, maybe *La La Land* would have. *Moonlight* could be seen as a protest vote, a rebuke to Trump, though it might have been that given the Academy's newly devised and complicated preferential-ballot system *Moonlight* had been backed more successfully than *La La Land* so maybe it wasn't *only* a protest vote.

He and I soon got into a conversation about ideology versus aesthetics, and how the entertainment press considered *Moonlight* first and foremost an ideological triumph, not simply an artistic one, though we both thought the latter claim was directly inflated by the prevailing ideology of the moment. We agreed that 2016 had been a terrible year for movies, and neither of us had cared passionately about any of the winners one way or the other, but our general debate led us briefly onto the topic of Black Lives Matter, since *Moonlight* obviously qualified due to the world into which it was released. But the difference, we argued, was that *Moonlight*'s aesthetics were sometimes exquisite while the *aesthetics* of Black Lives Matter were not. Perhaps if they had been, the movement could have reached the wider audience it wanted instead of turning off so many people. The Black Panthers' aesthetic grasp turned them into rock stars for young people, black and white, in the 1960s, but Black Lives Matter was a millennial mess with no sense at all of forming a coherent visual idea or style in presenting itself—and this culture presentation ends up being, for better or worse, everything. You would have to be a moral idiot not to recognize the movement's importance, but it was frustrating to see their message get eclipsed by a lurching, unformed aesthetic, and we noted that it could belong to the list of things on #WhyTrumpWon.

My female friend had been listening to us while drinking heavily and at this point she suddenly exploded into a spastic rage, telling us that she was disgusted to hear two white men faulting the aesthetics of Black Lives Matter (which we'd done for about thirty seconds) and that we were both guilty of "white male privilege" and what in the fuck were we talking about? Trump *hadn't* won the election, and she couldn't bear sitting at the table listening to members of the "white patriarchy" rip apart the aesthetics of such an essential movement. "What?" she asked. "You want the Black Lives girls to be *thinner*? Is that what you're implying?" What she actually was implying was the sentimental narrative that said white men shouldn't be allowed to privately criticize anything about Black Lives Matter. She kept ranting, often nonsensically, and though I'd known her for more than thirty years I'd never seen her so angry, so deranged, talking right over us when we tried to explain what we meant, as if it needed any clarifying. We finally calmed her down, but our dinner had already been ruined by the outburst. Though we all kept it together for the rest of the evening, the frustration I felt seemed familiar: a continuation of the knee-jerk overemotional lashing out that had become endemic in the culture when it came to Trump, and particularly viral among the morally superior *wealthy* people I knew: coastal Democrats whose bubble lives the election had burst apart. This friend of mine lived in a penthouse with stunning views of Central Park and probably had a net worth of more than ten million dollars, so I kept wondering why her vast misery was all Trump's fault? How had she let this happen to herself? Where were these cries of indignation coming from? Had Trump made her act like a sloppy mess by relentlessly victimizing and antagonizing *her*? And what about the almost sixty-three million people who'd voted for him? Were they also making her sick?

■ ■ ■

Barbra Streisand told the media she was gaining weight because of Trump. Lena Dunham told the media she was losing weight because of Trump. People everywhere were now blaming the president for their own problems and neuroses. This happened again when Meryl Streep accepted her lifetime achievement award at the Golden Globes in January 2017, and rather than paying tribute to all the filmmakers she'd worked with who had passed away in the last few years (Michael Cimino, Mike Nichols, Nora Ephron) or—especially—talking about what playing Carrie Fisher in *Postcards from the Edge* was like, since Fisher had died just two weeks earlier, she used this opportunity to go on an anti-Trump rant for ten minutes. Instead of eulogizing her friend, she'd reinstated the new corporate moral superiority and ignored the aesthetics of the occasion by pushing her own ideology. But it wasn't a surprise, really, since this is a company town, and in the waning days of February I was again reminded why I didn't go out much in LA when I attended a pre-Oscars party where two wealthy players at our dinner table spent the entire time complaining about Trump. One of them had worked with Steve Bannon during his Hollywood days, and in fact he showed us a text he'd just got from Bannon, then the White House's chief strategist, noting that if his wife ever found out he was going to *text* Bannon *back* she would probably divorce him and take the kids. That sounded extreme to me, and I jokingly said so. But he was serious and stared at me sternly when he explained that his wife had been having "breakdowns" ever since the inauguration. Yet, during the awards season of 2017, a month after that inauguration, while the rich man's wife was having breakdowns in a palace on a hillside, no one ever acknowledged that a small district in Beverly Hills, its northwestern edge spanning Sunset Boulevard, had actually been carried by Trump—the only red district in La La Land's sea of blue. How could anyone fit this into a neat, sentimental narrative? The outrage, indignation, panic and horror of the Trump Apocalypse was really just the manifestation of being forced to look at the underlying bubble and wonder in shame where it all went wrong.

■ ■ ■

The agony and the self-victimizing were still going strong in the spring of 2017, at yet another dinner I had with another two friends I hadn't seen since the election—both men in their sixties and privy to vast fortunes. Drinks had just been ordered when one of them muttered darkly about whatever Trump had "fucked up" that day. When I countered with something noncommit- tal about the day's events or perhaps offered another opinion, placing the supposed fuckup in context, they both lost their shit and became infuriated, lashing out at me in ways I'd never seen from either of them. I had known one of them for more than thirty years—we'd met when I was twenty-one—and I had never seen him this apoplectic before, and in a swirl of morally superior self-regard and indignation he started *lecturing* me until I was ultimately hounded to say okay, forget it, you're right, you're *both* right, just forget all about it. Later, after both men opined that Trump actually *hadn't* won the election, I mentioned the Electoral College—and they immediately shot back that the Electoral College shouldn't count, either. One of them said the Electoral College was "bullshit" and that Los Angeles and New York *should* determine who "the fucking president" is. "I don't want any goddamn know-nothing rural hicks deciding who the president should be," he growled. "I *am* a proud liberal coastal elite and I think *we* should pick the president because *we know better.*" My blood froze, or at least I went cold, when I heard this, and it certainly wasn't what Clinton's advisers Robby Mook and John Podesta had said when Trump called the Electoral College "a rigged thing" and "a fraud," suggesting that maybe only the popular vote should matter. I was going to point this out just because their outrage was so over-the-top annoying but then backed down, pretending to be the contrarian in order to mollify them, even though I actually thought I was the only one who was being logical about this. I was never good at playing the alpha dog, anyway.

■ ■ ■

Halfway through the campaign, I'd noticed I was no longer reading only the *Times*, or watching only CNN and MSNBC; I was also checking out Fox and other conservative newsfeeds (including Breitbart) and realizing with harsh disbelief that we were living in two totally different worlds that I'd never bothered to notice before, inside two worlds that didn't even come close to overlapping, and I felt naïve for failing to grasp the stark contrast until now. But why was one considered "right" and the other "wrong"?—where were these absolutes coming from? Were Trump's supporters *only* deplorables and alt-right racists? Were Clinton's *really* out-of-touch neoliberal elitists who didn't care about anything except identity politics and the corporate status quo? Talking to anybody about the election in that darkening summer and fall of 2016, you'd have thought there was nothing centrist about how people chose to cast their vote, and that no coming together would be allowed; the idea of healing, of mending, seemed impossible. You were either virtue voting for one candidate or voting for the other and therefore evil. The women I knew who were for Trump were all about the economy and immigration, and they resented that gender supposedly forced them to line up behind a candidate they didn't believe in. And in Los Angeles they learned the hard way that if they admitted this, massive wide-eyed disbelief followed by arguments would ensue, started by people they saw as overly sensitive and out-of-touch elitists; since any conversation would tank, they kept quiet. It was an insurmountable headache.

In February 2016, months before Trump won the primary, I had dinner with two youngish couples in their late thirties, one of whom I'd known for about a decade, and the other I met that night in a West Hollywood restaurant. I had never talked politics with the couple I had known for ten years because I wasn't interested and assumed they weren't either, though I knew they'd voted for Obama in both 2008 and 2012. During the second round of cocktails things loosened up and someone mentioned uncritically something that Trump had said in a speech earlier that week and a surprising and dramatic hesitancy suddenly landed on the table. We all looked at one other, sipping our drinks, before one of the women, a small-business owner, confessed that she liked Trump, and was going to vote for him, with her husband agreeing, much to the relief of the other couple, who said they would as well. Even then, we were all certain Trump would be the Republican candidate, despite the legacy media assuring us that this was all but impossible, but I also knew at that dinner that I probably wouldn't be voting for him, or for Clinton. I was shocked by these two couples' announcement that they would be supporting Trump, but I wasn't *offended*. Instead, I became curious and started asking everyone why they'd moved from Obama to Trump. The reasons were mostly economic, having to do with trade and immigration, with political correctness and identity politics coming in a close third and fourth. In other words: these were white people.

■ ■ ■

That night I went home and tweeted about this surprising discovery: I actually *knew* people in Los Angeles who were backing Trump (and within a year I knew many more). By then it was eleven o'clock on a Saturday night and I thought the tweet was funny, and who'd be reading it anyway at this hour? It was just a lark, with the tweet saying only that I'd just gotten home from a dinner in West Hollywood and been shocked that the entire table was voting for Trump but weren't eager to admit it. Then I watched *Saturday Night Live* and went to bed. In the morning I woke up groggily, vaguely aware that the millennial lying next to me was already awake and looking at his phone. Silence reigned in the dark bedroom until he asked in a low voice, "Why in the hell did you tweet that last night?" I thought about it for a moment and then remembered what I'd tweeted. "Why?" I asked. I fumbled for my glasses as he showed me his phone, and I saw that the tweet had been retweeted thousands and thousands of times (unheard of for anything I'd ever tweeted), not least by Donald J. Trump himself. In fact the tweet made international news overnight, and was now being covered on hundreds of blogs, and media requests in America as well as in Europe began pouring in, all of which I turned down. Because what would I be promoting? What would I be defending? People on the left refused to believe that this had really happened and preferred to believe I was trolling everybody, and they doubted if *anyone* in that part of Los Angeles would vote for Trump, along with disbelief that any *women* there would either. Yet in the end that tiny district in Beverly Hills *did* vote for Trump as did 45 percent of college-educated white females and 62 percent of those not college educated. This was around the time that I began to lay off Twitter.

The woman I'd known for a decade texted me later that Sunday and said she'd laughed when she saw the tweet, but she also warned me not to ever mention who was at that dinner. Her business was Hollywood-based, and who knew what could happen in this divisive climate; she'd noticed that people were far too hysterical, and to defend your beliefs just wasn't worth the trouble. *What an awful way to live*, I thought. To ever behave like that would make me too stressed-out and exhausted, as a writer who had always considered himself liberal and a defender of free speech and a believer in people's rights to express themselves however they chose to and in any way they wanted. I was now looking at a new kind of liberalism, one that willingly censored people and punished voices, obstructed opinions and blocked viewpoints. This illiberalism was becoming the alarming norm, in the media, in Hollywood, and for a moment nowhere more glaringly than on college campuses in 2017, but this seemed to become the breaking point for everyone. The irony was amplified when students—and, it seemed, the institution's administration itself—rejected conservative speakers at *Berkeley*, once considered the bastion of free speech in America, and there was zero chance of spinning that story into an aspirational narrative for the Left or the Resistance or for anybody else anymore. All this was simply becoming embarrassing, and you could even sense the legacy media's hesitancy to cover it.

By then, you couldn't get around the idea that Hollywood and college campuses and the media were all deep seas of mixed signals and moral hypocrisy. Whatever the terrible reality of these businesses and corporations and organizations happened to *be*, that they would enforce *rules* about what artists and civilians should be able to say—which is what the friend who called me was worried about—was scary enough. But in the age of Trump there seemed to be no escape, no peace, for anybody. Rival views about *anything* had begun to feel like an attack on one's personal identity—even for those of us caught in the crossfire, who were strenuously independent—and everyone seemed vulnerable to micro-aggressions while living in their half of a black-and-white world. All I could think about hearing the voluminous din—of hatred, anger, shock—on either side of the divide was that it was time for everyone to pull on their big boy pants, have a stiff drink at the bar and start having true conversations, because ultimately we shared only one country. But that notion, too, had begun to sound sentimental.

■ ■ ■

In the winter of 2017, just a week after Trump's inauguration, I was in London giving a talk at the Royal Institute of Great Britain when I was asked by the moderator what I thought of the "unending horror" that was now happening in the United States. I had to stop him and clarify that this apocalyptic narrative about the election and the new president was really only that, a narrative, and merely a reflection of a vast epidemic of alarmist and catastrophic drama that American media was encouraging. I reminded the moderator that despite what he or I thought about Trump, roughly half of the people who had actually voted were somewhat happy with the results of the 2016 election. After I said this you could've heard a pin drop in the sold-out hall. Other things I said that were met with a deafening silence included that I didn't think Trump was going to be impeached; that the protests of the Resistance weren't going to change anything; that I defended the troublemaker Milo Yiannopoulos's right of free speech in an oversensitive corporate culture that was trying to muzzle him, and I admitted that I missed Milo's provocations on Twitter (he'd been kicked off) no matter how much I often disagreed with them, certainly more than I'd miss the tweets of a middle-aged comedienne who couldn't handle a vicious yet typical Twitter trolling and had been instrumental in getting him banned. Again, you could have heard the pins dropping. Nobody in the audience at the Royal Institute of Great Britain in the winter of 2017 wanted to hear any of this. At the signing afterward many people came up and were very polite, in that formal British style, and none of them said anything about my remarks except for a white man about my age who said he agreed with me about the protests. But my statements were considered so controversial that they made headlines in the *Irish Examiner* and *The Daily Mail* the following day. Somehow these opinions—they were merely that, not prophecies or facts—were provocative enough to warrant these headlines. The overreaction was alarmist, but that was the mood: in a post-Brexit UK there was a chill as well, especially given the realization that nationalism was beginning its sweep across Europe, blooming everywhere.

That same week in London, I was in the back of a cab when

the young American sitting across from me asked innocently what music I'd been listening to lately. As I thought about this it registered that my favorite pop music was being made by country artists: Jason Isbell, Miranda Lambert, Jamey Johnson, Brad Paisley, Kasey Musgrave, Ashley Monroe and Sturgill Simpson, among many others. One of my favorite songs of the past few years had been Luke Bryan's cotton-candy "Roller Coaster," the sort of nearly perfect pop production that wasn't being made anymore by actual pop stars. Country was the only place where you could find the pop-rock sweet spot that I was currently searching for—old-school rock and pop sounds and structures. Jason Isbell transcends country with his great *Southeastern* and *Something More Than Free* albums, but this young man hadn't heard of Jason Isbell. In fact he wasn't listening to any of the artists I mentioned. I'd known him for a little more than a year, and he was also a "survivor" of the election who'd turn into a sputtering wreck if Trump came up briefly in passing or his image was glimpsed on a screen or monitor, and he was shocked, and asked, seriously, how could I possibly like *that* music? I had no idea what the young man meant and I said so. And then he told me, "How can you like country music when they're all against us—don't you understand that? They are *against* us, Bret. Our values."

This was an educated white person, very successful in the high-end art world, and I stared at him without knowing how to respond. I had never gravitated toward any kind of music because of the politics it does or doesn't espouse: it's a question of whether I like the tunes or not, that's it. I explained this to the young man in that cab on a cold, wet London morning in the winter of 2017, but he didn't seem convinced. My liking country music confirmed something about me for him and suggested I was a traitor. I just smiled tightly as we arrived at our destination, and I remember wondering what the idealistic young American would think if I told him Jamey Johnson's *The Guitar Song* was a much better record than Kendrick Lamar's *To Pimp a Butterfly* and in that moment I suspected he would have been offended.

tweeting

For many of us who grew up in California, the American writer Joan Didion was a heroine even though, or because, she was a Goldwater Republican, she was in love with John Wayne, she thought Jim Morrison was sexy because he was a bad boy, she hated hippie culture, she hated the Beats, she hated '70s feminism, she idolized strong men in her fiction, she dismissed J. D. Salinger and Woody Allen when both were at the height of their popularity, she was the snob *and* the anti-snob. In short, she was fearlessly opinionated. In 1988 she wrote famously, obliquely, about where she stood politically at the end of the '80s: "It occurred to me during the summer of 1988, in California and Atlanta and New Orleans, in the course of watching first the California primary and then the Democratic and Republican national conventions, that it had not been by accident that the people with whom I had preferred to spend time in high school had, on the whole, hung out in gas stations." Many people disagreed with her stance on social issues, and she was fiercely criticized for an anti-feminism piece she wrote in 1972 called "The Women's Movement." ("That many women are victims of condescension and exploitation and sex-role stereotyping was scarcely news but neither was it news that other women are not: nobody forced women to buy the package.") But her style, her aesthetic, sold everything she wrote, and this belief in style, and the precision of her writing, seemingly erased ideology: she was a realist, a pragmatist, attuned to logic and facts, but a stylist *first*—as with all great writers, the style was where you located the meaning in her work. She had rejected the notion that as a woman she wasn't strong enough to deal with what she saw as the abrasiveness of daily life in a male-dominated society. And she also found something ominous at work in the feminist movement, beyond its objection to being discriminated against. "Increasingly it seemed that the aversion was to adult sexual life itself: how much cleaner to stay children forever."

This particular wish—the desire to remain a child forever—strikes me as a defining aspect in American life right now: a collective sentiment that imposes itself over the neutrality of facts and context. This narrative is about how we wish the world worked out in contrast to the disappointment that everyday life offers us, and it helps us to shield ourselves from not only the chaos of reality but also from our own personal failures. The sentimental narrative is a take on what Didion meant when she wrote that "we tell ourselves stories in order to live" in her famous essay "The White Album," from 1979. "The princess is caged in the consulate. The man with the candy will lead the children into the sea. The naked woman on the ledge outside the window on the sixteenth floor is a victim of accidie, or the naked woman is an exhibitionist, and it would be 'interesting' to know which. We tell ourselves that it makes some difference whether the naked woman is about to commit a mortal sin or is about to register a political protest or is about to be, the Aristophanic view, snatched back to the human condition by the fireman in priest's clothing just visible in the window behind her, the one smiling at the telephoto lens. We look for the sermon in the suicide, for the social or moral lesson in the murder of five. We interpret what we see, select the most workable of the multiple choices. We live entirely, especially if we are writers, by the imposition of a narrative line upon disparate images, by the 'ideas' with which we have learned to freeze the shifting phantasmagoria which is our actual experience."

The key phrase here is "especially if we are writers" because it seems that everyone has fallen under the thrall of this idea that we're all writers and dramatists now, that each of us has a special voice and something very important to say, usually about a *feeling* we have, and all this gets expressed in the black maw of social media billions of times a day. Usually this feeling is outrage, because outrage gets attention, outrage gets clicks, outrage can make your voice heard above the deafening din of voices squalling over one another in this nightmarish new culture—and the outrage is often tied to a lunacy demanding human perfection, spotless citizens, clean and likable comrades, and requiring thousands of apologies daily. Advocating while creating your own drama and your brand is where the game is now. And if you don't follow the new corporate rules accordingly you are banished, exiled, erased from history.

■ ■ ■

David Foster Wallace and I never met, but over the '90s and into the 2000s we often exchanged pleasantries through foreign journalists who were crisscrossing the country to interview youngish American writers. "Who are you interviewing next?" "David Foster Wallace." "Tell David I say hi." Or "Oh, by the way,

David Foster Wallace says hello." Wallace had been a fan of *Less Than Zero,* and yet I'd been amused by David's interpretation of *American Psycho* as "Neiman-Marcus nihilism" and never remotely felt we were having any kind of literary feud. We were still saying our distant hellos to each other *after* he made the *American Psycho* comments. But this was the full extent of our relationship, which is perhaps how it should have been since I couldn't get through his 1996 novel *Infinite Jest,* despite trying to a few times, and found his journalism bloated and minor-key condescending, and thought his Kenyon commencement speech from 2005 was a very special example of bullshit. I sensed the canonization following his suicide in 2008 to be based on a particular and very American sort of sentimental narrative, yet a film about Wallace released in 2015, *The End of the Tour,* was surprisingly easy to take even though it's reverential to a fault. Smoothly directed by James Ponsoldt and elegantly written by the playwright Donald Margulies, the movie is often as static as filmed plays can be—with long stretches of dialogue that essentially constitute a debate about *authenticity*—and you can either get stoned on all of the goodwill at hand or roll your eyes in disbelief that this was actually taken as seriously and presented as laboriously as it seems to have been by everybody involved. *The End of the Tour* stars Jason Segel as Wallace and Jesse Eisenberg as David Lipsky, a *Rolling Stone* journalist who tags along at the end of Wallace's U.S. book tour for *Infinite Jest,* and for those of us who were also touring and immersed in publishing in the 1990s, the movie provides a comically accurate account of a Gen-X era that is long gone: Walter Kirn's book reviews in *New York* magazine ignite entire party conversations, *Rolling Stone* commissions a profile of an avant-garde academic novelist, people in cars sing along to Alanis Morissette anthems and smoking's allowed everywhere. The digital age had not yet fully arrived.

The movie's adapted from Lipsky's book *Although of Course You End Up Becoming Yourself*, which was published two years after Wallace hung himself. *Rolling Stone* never published Lipsky's profile, and the book consists solely of the transcripts of the conversations he and Wallace had over five days in 1996, chiefly about one's *genuine* self versus the self that worries about how an audience assembles a false you from your fiction, and about how what they have read shades into a construction of who they think you are. In the movie, Wallace is presented as a guy who was just too sensitive for this world, which strikes a certain emotional chord with younger viewers and especially actors. He's portrayed as an angelic Pop-Tart-sharing schlub, a heartwarming populist, a tortured everyman who loves dogs and kids and McDonald's, who exudes "realness" and "humanity." But the movie completely omits any reference to the *other* Wallace: the contemptuous one, the contrarian, the jealous asshole with a violent side, the cruel critic—all the things some of us found interesting about him. This movie prefers Saint David of the Kenyon commencement called "This Is Water: Some Thoughts Delivered on a Significant Occasion, about Living a Compassionate Life," a speech some of his staunchest defenders and even former editors have a hard time stomaching, arguing that it's the worst thing Wallace ever wrote, but which became a mini viral sensation. *This* Wallace is the voice of reason, a sage, and the movie succumbs to the cult of likability, but the *real* David scolded people and probably craved fame—and it's hardly rare that writers are both suspicious of literary acclaim and curious to see how that game's played out. Wallace was cranky and could be mean and caustic, but this David

Foster Wallace is erased, which is why the movie is so resolutely one-note and earnest.

■ ■ ■

This isn't the David Foster Wallace who voted for Reagan and supported Ross Perot, who wrote a scathing and deliciously cruel putdown of late-period John Updike, who posed for glamour-puss photos in *Interview* magazine (years before *Infinite Jest*) and appeared on Charlie Rose's show a couple of times—all of which *The End of the Tour* strongly suggests was absolute agony for the David who keeps naïvely fretting about his real self being co-opted by a fake self, as if a man as intelligent as he was would really care one way or the other. I admire David Foster Wallace's ambition and talent and wide-ranging literary experimentalism, even though for the most part I thought he was a fake-out artist whose disingenuous personality belied his genuine complexity. (See, for instance, his remark that "AIDS's gift to us lies in its loud reminder that there's nothing casual about sex at all"—a line I would've loved to have seen Jason Segel's puppy dog David try to deliver sincerely.) It's the rewritten construct of what Wallace *became*—misinterpreted by a generation of fans who see him as a hip motivational speaker and most importantly a *victim*—that is the central problem: the masking of an actual man in favor of a figure many of them don't mind and seem, in fact, to prefer.

The very thing that Wallace always feared might happen to him is happily encouraged and actualized by *The End of the Tour*, and it's kind of mind-blowing that the movie either didn't figure this out or chose to simply ignore it. Minute by minute, scene by scene, the film rejects everything David Foster Wallace supposedly stood for and believed in. It's a massive contradiction that leaves one somewhat dumbfounded by the adolescent hubris of both the portrayal and the conception, which seems determined to deliver something that its star keeps saying he doesn't want—to become a character—and the movie willfully ignores this complaint. This is what the Wallace in the film is bothered by in scene after scene after scene—and what does the movie do? It keeps filming him. And what does *Segal* do? He keeps playing a particular *idea* of David Foster Wallace, which is why the movie would have driven Wallace insane. The Wallace estate as well as his editor have disavowed the film, not because it gets anything factually wrong but because it does exactly what Wallace never would've tolerated: it turns him into an actor. "Be a good guy," Wallace begs Lipsky in their last scene in *The End of the Tour*, taking him to task, almost pleading, and though this might be an honorable way to live your life as a bro, it's a *terrible* idea for a writer.

■ ■ ■

Wallace didn't start writing fiction until he was twenty-one. The origin story is that he purportedly saw the success of the literary Brat Pack, and of other young novelists who started selling books and making money in the mid-'80s, and thought, *Why not give it a shot?* There are traces of *Less Than Zero*'s influence in his first novel, *The Broom of the System*—though he later disavowed this influence even as he continued to publicly praise *Less Than Zero*. I went on a Twitter rant a few years ago—caused by a mix of insomnia and tequila—when I was reading D. T. Max's biography of Wallace. This rant had less to do with David than his growing audience, who were conflating the suicide and the Kenyon address into an aspirational narrative that—if you'd read everything by and about Wallace, and had followed his trajectory—felt abjectly sentimental. As with many of the peers who interested me, I had read all of David's work (except, of course, for *Infinite Jest*, which I hadn't been able to find a way into despite its snazzy and prescient central idea of corporations taking over the American entertainment industry) and, except for a few early stories and sections from *The Broom of the System*, I failed to connect with his work for numerous aesthetic reasons. I often considered David the most overrated writer of our generation, as well as the most pretentious and tortured, and tweeted as much that night along with other things that bothered me, including how the culture had reinterpreted him and how naïve I thought David was to believe he could control this. The sincerity and the earnestness he began trafficking in seemed to some of us a ploy, a kind of contradiction—not totally fake, but not totally real either, a kind of performance art in which he'd sensed the societal shift toward earnestness and accommodated himself to it. But I still liked the *idea* of David and the fact that he existed, and I also think he was a genius.

While my feelings about him were—yes—contradictory, they were also honest. An increasing problem in our society is people's inability to bear two opposing thoughts in mind at the same time, so that any "criticism" of someone's work is routinely blamed as feelings of elitism, or feelings of jealousy or superiority. The notion of pushing the "like" button on everything, of shutting people down for voicing differing opinions is something Wallace would have certainly bristled at, since he could be a demanding, even decimating, critic himself. Predictably, people reacted to the late-night tweets (I had misspelled "douche bag") with how-dare-you outrage and labeled me a hater and a jealous troll. But I didn't have any personal problems with David and was never jealous of him; the tweets were more of a tirade against fans who'd ignored the negative and unpleasant aspects of his life and willfully pretended that the sometimes cruel dick who walked among us had never existed. There wasn't anything David wrote that I was ever envious of, because our work had nothing in common with each other's in style or content or temperament. (However, Jonathan Franzen's another story, and *The Corrections* is a novel I've often said that I wished I'd written.) This tweetfest was merely an aesthetic judgment—an opinion—that somehow registered as a crime.

■ ■ ■

In an appreciation of the pop singer Sky Ferreira for the *LA Weekly* in the summer of 2016 the young writer Art Tavana rhapsodized:

> Sky Ferreira has a name that reads like a turbo-charged Italian sports car, or the kindred spirit to second generation Italian-American pop-star Madonna, the most ambitious woman to ever wear a pink cone bra. Both Sky and Madonna have similar breasts in both cup size

> and ability to cause a shitstorm . . . America has already established that Ferreira looks a lot like Madonna but we almost never have the audacity to admit that her looks offer the most appeal to the American consumer. To pretend looks don't matter in pop music is ridiculous. Looks matter, they always will.

Tavana then went on to describe how Ferreira had moved past this idea: "She's too nasty to be anyone's schoolgirl fantasy . . . She's the pop star who's so personally cool that her record label Capitol doesn't need to hire a team to mold her."

Tavana praised Ferreira as a fashion icon and an accomplished actress and related how she was hated by elitist snobs in the indie scene and decried by feminists when she refused to condemn the photographer Terry Richardson, an accused pornographer and misogynist, adding that she never let her past history of sexual abuse define her. Tavana also pointed out how pop stars profit off their beauty, and that their sexual allure attracts fans. The piece reminded me of how when Blondie broke through, so many guys in my high school who hadn't been particularly interested in New Wave suddenly started drooling over Deborah Harry and turned into big fans of it all, even ignoring previous favorites like the Eagles and Foreigner. The same thing happened again with Patty Smyth and Scandal, and later on with Susannah Hoffs and the Bangles. But this looks-ism goes back to Elvis Presley's beauty and to the Beatles and Mick Jagger and Jim Morrison and Sting and every single boy band that ever existed, yet somehow there's still something different about these male and female narratives.

Women are looked at and judged and appropriated or demeaned a lot more frequently than men will ever be, but in an era driven by the dreaded idea of inclusivity for everyone, no matter what, beauty now seems threatening, a separator, a divider, instead of just a natural thing: people who are admired and desired for their looks, individuals stepping away from the herd and being worshipped for their beauty. For many of us this is a reminder of our own physical inadequacies in the face of what our culture defines as sexy, beautiful, hot—and yes, men will be men, boys will be boys, and dudes will be dudes, and nothing's ever going to change that. But to pretend that looks and hotness, whether you're a guy or a girl, shouldn't make you popular is one of those sad stances that can make you question the validity, or the reality, of this cult of inclusivity. Tavana's ode to Sky Ferreira might not have been especially well written, though it was clearly an honest account by a man who was looking at a woman he might have desired and writing about that desire, even as it overshadowed what he thought about her music. So the question became: What if he's honest about objectifying her?

Social-justice warriors from *LAist*, *Flavorwire*, *Jezebel*, *Teen Vogue* and *Vulture* couldn't let this innocuous piece go unnoticed without throwing hissy fits, and so pissed-off and supposedly offended that they were *obliged* to denounce Art Tavana. When reading similar pieces by young journalists, some of whom should've known better, I wondered when liberal progressives had become such society matrons, clutching their pearls in horror every time anyone had an opinion that wasn't the mirror image of their own. The high moral tone seized by social-justice warriors, and increasingly an unhinged Left, is always out of scale with whatever they're actually indignant about, and I wasn't surprised that this hideous and probably nerve-wracking tendency had begun to create an authoritarian language police. *Teen Vogue* found the use of "boobs" and "knockers" *misogynistic* and lodged a rather insipid complaint about the male gaze. Whenever I hear an objection to the male gaze—hoping that it will . . . what? Go away, get rerouted, become contained—I automatically think, *Are people really this deluded and deranged or haven't they had a date in the last ten years?* The writer piping up in *Teen Vogue* about Tavana's insensitive misogyny then lectured us that women needed to be respected and not judged by their looks—and yes, the irony was delicious coming from *Teen Vogue*—and it sounded pretty childish, as did all the other commentators across social media by saying he'd "reduced a woman's art to whether you want to fuck her or not" or, more directly, "You're trash—fuck you." (I couldn't help but wonder what Joan Didion would have made of all this.) There was also the suggestion in some of these pieces that Tavana knew exactly what he was doing—inciting feminist hysteria to see if these people would take the bait, and that maybe he didn't find Ferreira attractive at all, which was what he hinted at later when questioned about the piece. But, of course, they always take the bait.

■ ■ ■

I also kept wondering, throughout that week in the summer of 2016, what if all I wanted to do was bang Nick Jonas (a question still) and maybe wrote a fifteen-hundred-word ode, talking about his chest and his ass and his dumb-sexy face and the fact I didn't really like his music—would that have been a dis on Nick? Or what if a woman wanted to write about how she really hated if we want to function as a free-speech society that believes—or even pretends to—in the First Amendment. At the same time, I never really believed that *Jezebel* or *Flavorwire* cared about any of this. Did they actually want to vilify a man for confessing that maybe he thinks Sky Ferreira's *hot*? Or were they just venting away in the continuous vacuum of their own invention? By now, just months before the election, it truly felt we were entering into an authoritarian cultural moment fostered by the Left—what had once been my side of the aisle, though I couldn't even recognize it anymore. How had this happened? It seemed so regressive and grim and childishly unreal, like a dystopian sci-fi movie in which you can express yourself only in some neutered form, a mound, or a clump of flesh and cells, turning away from your gender-based responses to women, to men, to sex, to even *looking*. This castration was something no one really hoped for, I didn't think, during that summer—but maybe everyone was willing to go along with it because it might fill a column or two, and who didn't need a little more clickbait?

■ ■ ■

Back in 2015 on my podcast I began talking about ideology versus aesthetics in the arts and how one seemed to be trumping the other just then in terms of reactions from the media and certain factions of the Left. "Look at the art, not the artist." The first time I heard that line was in an interview with Bruce Springsteen about thirty years ago, and it has stayed with me ever since. (That this hero of mine would later get Trumped by releasing his worst

Drake's music but found him so physically hot and desirable that she was lusting for him anyway? Where would that put her? Where would that put *me*? Would either of these pieces raise any eyebrows? Were we then equal? No, not even close, because in our culture social-justice warriors always prefer women to be *victims.* The responses from *Jezebel* and *Flavorwire* and *Teen Vogue* all recast Ferreira as a victim, reinforcing her (supposed) violation at the hands of a male writer—the usual hall-of-mirrors loop people find themselves in when looking for something, anything, to get angry about, and one where they can occasionally, eventually, get tripped up. The reality is that men look at women, and men look at other men, and women look at men, and women especially size up other women and objectify them. Has anybody who's ever been on a dating app recently *not* seen how our Darwinian impulses are gratified by a swipe or two? This, in order for our species to survive, is the way of the world and it's never going to be modified or erased. I somehow knew, during that week, that this fake controversy, which seemed both misguided and pompous, would blow over in about twenty-four hours, and that ideally Ferreira might have defended the *LA Weekly* piece—though she never did. What bothered me most was that since Tavana's article was only his *opinion,* why were people getting so outraged about it?

The sad ending of this story was that the *LA Weekly,* which had edited and posted the piece, felt they needed to *apologize* for it in the wake of all the online howling—for a piece where someone had clearly written honestly, sometimes embarrassingly so, about an entertainer and how he judged her. That was it. That should be allowed. The overreaction epidemic that's rampant in our society, as well as the specter of censorship, should *not* be allowed single ever—the anti-Trump rant called "That's What Makes Us Great"—was one of the cultural low points in 2017.) Art should stand as the artist's truth, and the artists themselves? Well, you'll probably be disappointed so just look at the art and let that speak for itself. Yet now Springsteen's remark had started to sound like an antiquated slogan, something only a man of a certain age (either a boomer or one of the first Gen Xers) would believe in, because we were constantly being reminded that this was now supposedly a different world altogether—and, more chillingly, we were told, an "enlightened" and "progressive" one that fully acknowledged our "identities"—even while there was so much evidence that didn't support this claim. To me, it seemed like a highly reductive view. But I also realized that certain reevaluations had occurred to me when I saw how people responded to my own identity as an artist—and, therefore, to my work.

That summer, *The New York Times* asked me to profile Quentin Tarantino. I hadn't written a celebrity profile in more than twenty years, when I'd happened to be stranded in LA for a couple of months, drifting through the writing and preplanning for a movie that never happened, and *Details* magazine had asked me if I wanted to profile Val Kilmer, who was then shooting *Batman Forever* on the Warner Bros. lot and starring as Bruce Wayne. Because I was bored by waiting around, and because of how much money the magazine offered me (an outrageous sum that doesn't exist anymore), I agreed to do it even though I didn't find Kilmer especially interesting, and this impression wasn't transformed by the following events: lunch at a deserted sushi bar off Mulholland one afternoon; in Kilmer's trailer on the Warner Bros. lot, with Kilmer in full Batman makeup and regalia, lolling around smoking cigarettes and pontificating as I fumbled with my tape recorder; on a late-Friday-night drive out to Culver City, where we talked while stuck in traffic on the 405; and finally in another trailer while he endured makeup tests for his upcoming role in Michael Mann's *Heat,* which was shooting nearby. The piece had turned out okay, but the arguments with the editor over cuts and omissions, as well as information concerning Kilmer's love life that I *hadn't even written* added into the piece, forced me to ask myself why I'd consider anything like this ever again.

But *The New York Times* enticed me by clarifying what they had in mind: the *T Magazine* supplement was putting together an issue called *The Greats* with various writers covering various cultural figures who were hovering in that cultural moment: Rihanna, Jonathan Franzen, the filmmaker Steve McQueen, Karl Lagerfeld and Tarantino. I said yes because I actually *was* interested in Tarantino: in his films, in a Gen-X sensibility we both shared, and in the man himself, who seemingly knew more about film history than any other middle-aged American auteur. I admired how, in interviews, he was fearlessly opinionated about actors, directors, movies and TV series. I hate saying "fearlessly," since that hardly describes dissing Oscar-bait movies or saying you don't care for Cate Blanchett or that you found the first season of *True Detective* really boring after watching only one episode. There was once what now seems a magical moment where you could voice your opinions, make them public and commence a genuine discussion, but the culture now seemed so fearful of discourse that any such thing instead provokes an attack, which is precisely what happened when *The New York Times* published the Tarantino piece.

I'd met Tarantino only twice, which seemed strange since

we had many acquaintances in common. He was now heavily into editing *The Hateful Eight*, which was opening that December, and barely had time for any interviews. While mine would amount to a tiny twenty-five-hundred-word mini-profile, the magazine thought it was essential to have the writer spend *some* face time with the subject, and I ended up talking to Tarantino for two hours at his house in the Hollywood Hills, before he drove us to the revival theater he owns, the New Beverly, to watch a Chaplin movie. Afterward he wanted to get something to eat, but it was nearing eleven and I had a meeting the next morning, so we said our goodbyes. I really liked Tarantino: generous, friendly, good-natured, approachable and endlessly smart about movies. His genuine love of the medium is especially infectious when you're hanging together, and he's also a tough, clear-eyed critic. Our interview was actually just a conversation, not a hard-hitting investigation of Tarantino and his films—just a few soft-lob questions about a couple of things I was curious about that we explored over a bottle of red wine while sitting by the pool in his backyard. I wrote the piece quickly, but when the deadline approached I couldn't see how to cut it down. I'd turned in double what they asked for, and of course they ran their favorite half. I knew that Tarantino's monologue on his black critics post–*Django Unchained* might push a few buttons, but it also seemed fair and benign, though I would have preferred to leave in the paragraph where he'd talked about his now-complicated feelings for his youthful hero-crush Jean-Luc Godard, or his takedown of Hitchcock, whom Tarantino had never really liked. In fact, Tarantino's admission that he preferred Gus Van Sant's remake of *Psycho* over the original was the most shocking thing in the transcript.

■ ■ ■

So, what were the two things that Tarantino said that were so appalling, disrespectful, sick-making, sexist, racist, and newsworthy that social media erupted with thousands of outraged souls calling for his severed head? One was reference to *Inglourious Basterds* losing to Kathryn Bigelow's *The Hurt Locker* at the 2010 Oscars in the categories of picture, director, and original screenplay, and here it is verbatim: "The Kathryn Bigelow thing—I got it. Look, it was exciting that a woman had made such a good war film, and it was the first movie about the Iraq War that said something. And it wasn't like I lost to something dreadful. It's not like *E.T.* losing to *Gandhi*." And the second was about the supposed Oscars snubbing of Ava DuVernay and her Martin Luther King biopic *Selma* during the 2015 awards season; many people in LA didn't respond to the movie for aesthetic reasons, yet the entertainment press acted stunned and outraged that it received no nominations for director, actor, screenplay—ideology run amok. Here's all that Tarantino had to say about this: "She [DuVernay] did a very good job on *Selma*, but *Selma* deserved an Emmy." Tarantino was parroting a typical response to the film within the Hollywood community—that it seemed like a TV movie—but he had actually gone on the record with it. Throughout the conversation I taped that night he'd also given his honest thoughts about various male filmmakers as well, and though some of these were cut from the piece they weren't all favorable either.

But the internet exploded, and a day later there had been hundreds if not thousands of complaints worldwide that Tarantino was an outrageous sexist and an uninhibited racist for making those two statements—and I wasn't far behind for endorsing him and for writing the profile. Tarantino was punished for "attacking" Bigelow and DuVernay—*two women!*—even though he had treated them neutrally, like adults, like the male filmmakers he also had issues with. What was disturbing about this reaction was, again, that it had formed itself against an *opinion.* As with Tavana's Ferreira piece, a demand was issued suggesting that on the basis of an ideology—because those under discussion were women and/or black—artists needed to be protected from freedom of speech. The outrage directed at Tarantino turned Bigelow and DuVernay into victims. While he'd simply offered his assessments of two movies, the disproportion of the response turned these artists into martyrs, and ironically, in doing so, *disempowered* both of them. Social-justice warriors never think like artists; they're looking only to be offended, not provoked or inspired, and often by nothing at all. When a few months later I tweeted admiringly about Saoirse Ronan's performance in *Brooklyn,* calling it the best performance I'd seen by any actor that year, complimenting its unfussiness, directness, and how luminous it was, and saying that it had no vanity, I noticed that a few women tried to turn my compliment ("no vanity") into an insult by implying, in essence, that I was "fat-shaming" Ronan.

■ ■ ■

I'd sparked my own Kathryn Bigelow "moment" already, when on December 5, 2012, at 11:31 p.m. I tweeted that "Kathryn Bigelow would be considered a mildly interesting filmmaker if she was a man but since she's a very hot woman she's really overrated."

This was my Twitter-casual response, half jokey, half not, after both the National Board of Review and the New York Film Critics Circle named her the best director of the year, and her new movie—*Zero Dark Thirty*, which was about the ten-year hunt for Osama Bin Laden—the best picture. I hadn't seen *Zero Dark Thirty* at the time (it hadn't opened, and screeners weren't available yet), but I thought, directly as I typed: Can a Kathryn Bigelow movie be *that* good or was something else at play that had to do with ideology and representation? She and Marc Boal, the screenwriter of *The Hurt Locker*, had collaborated again, and everything about this team's previous effort had seemed to me not bad exactly, but middle of the road, simplistic, visually standard: a war movie that lacked madness. Interestingly, *The Hurt Locker* also, I thought, felt like it had been—within the mainstream American movie system—directed generically by a man. Its testosterone level was palpable, whereas in the work of Sofia Coppola, Andrea Arnold, Jane Campion, Mia Hansen-Love, or Claire Denis you were aware of a much different presence behind the camera. *The Hurt Locker*, however, could have been directed by any gender, which is why it probably won the Oscar.

That same night in late 2012, I went on and tweeted this: "Kathryn Bigelow: Strange Days, K-19 The Widowmaker, Blue Steel, The Hurt Locker. Are we talking about visionary filmmaking or just OK junk?" The only thing that bothers me slightly about that tweet is the use of the word "junk," because the movies listed above are hardly junk when compared to the other big American studio movies during the period she was making them. Bigelow's craftsmanship level is often quite high, and these films are certainly ambitious and have a hardness and unsentimentality that's rare in studio pictures, as well as that curious anonymity noted above. They might be just "OK" overall, though they're certainly not "junk" in terms of their formal rigor and execution—messed-up scripts, perhaps, but my "junk" in that tweet is just the writer's exclamation point, a Twitter flourish. I didn't really like any of those films, and except for that one word I'm fine with the tweet, which isn't gender-specific. It's specifically about Bigelow's work and not about her identity.

The next day, December 6, I tweeted, "Concerned Empire woman offended by Bigelow tweets writes 'I love you, babe. But stop tweeting wasted.' When the hell else should I tweet?!?" This friend, an Oscar-nominated producer, had called me out earlier that day about my previous tweets and by now was laughing about her own panicked self-seriousness. She was more worried, I think, about repercussions from the entertainment press. Even though she knew I was comfortable with getting bashed in the Twittersphere, she was still concerned about the legacy media and how they would undoubtedly, inevitably trash me yet again. As if this hadn't been going on for years. The most recent instance was due to the fact that for months I'd been campaigning on Twitter for the *Fifty Shades of Grey* screenwriting gig. And then, when I didn't get it, complained about the writer who was eventually hired (we later became friends). So now I was "ungentlemanly" and a "sore loser," and therefore "we must take Twitter away from Bret Easton Ellis." That Twitter campaign had been partly sincere and partly performance art, and like everything, I thought, in the immediate Twitter moment, meant to be surprising, playful *and* provocative, real *and* fake, easy to read *and* hard to decipher, and most importantly, *not to be taken too seriously.*

■ ■ ■

Some of the outrage over the tweets certainly stemmed from an interview in 2010 I gave to a *Movieline* reporter while promoting my latest book, when the following happened over drinks at the Soho House in West Hollywood. The majority of our conversation revolved around movies, and at one point he asked what my favorite recent movies were. After thinking about it, I realized the answer was Andrea Arnold's *Fish Tank* and Floria Sigismondi's *The Runaways*, and I remembered that I'd tweeted, surprised by how powerful Arnold's film was, "Best movie I've seen in a year and I've gotta stop saying women can't direct" and promptly told the reporter about all this. We then were struck by a subsequent question: Where were all the *other* women directors? Both of us had multiple drinks that evening—this would be my last interview where alcohol was involved—and, buzzed, I started pontificating on why there weren't more female directors. It was actually a searching conversation where I theorized that maybe it's a medium more suited to men—its nerd-geek technicality, the ruthless rapidity of images, the voyeuristic quality that's the essence of the best moviemaking and the aggressiveness of making *any* movie, at least within the confines of American moviemaking—and suggested that there was a credible difference in the way men and women create films. (As the film historian and critic David Thomson has asked: "What are movies without male lust?") Some of this made it into the article, and some didn't. Some of it seems dumb in today's context, but this wasn't an academic's published thesis, just a somewhat drunken conversation where I actually said that the few movies made by women didn't have the violence, the technical virtuosity or the wild reckless imbalance that I was looking for, as those made by men—so what's up? Predictably I got slammed for saying that in 2010, and making those remarks has sometimes haunted me ever since. Remarks I've discussed in detail on my podcast with female directors Illeana Douglas and Rose McGowan and Karyn Kusama, who directed my favorite American movie of 2016, *The Invitation*.

■ ■ ■

On December 7 I kept it up: "Barraged today by people who think I'm 'sexist' and 'toxic' for thinking the beautiful Kathryn Bigelow is overrated because she's a woman." Now I was trolling. And my desire was to have a good time, to be a provocative, somewhat outrageous and opinionated critic, to be a bad boy, a douche, to lead my own dance in this writers' funhouse—all in 140 characters or less—and it became a problem for my Twitter self. The last thing Twitter seemed good for was to be "sensitive" about anything, and I was often at odds with the notion that anyone could really, deeply *care* about a Tweet in the first place. You tweeted, people screamed, people laughed, you shrugged, everyone moved on—that's how I initially saw Twitter. But after a while I realized that Twitter actually *encouraged* anger and despair—from the overly sincere, the virtue signaler, the dumb-ass, the literal-minded, the humorless. Until then I'd never considered it as a place to define your moral authority, or grab respect, or show off your most sensible assets. Twitter was about flashing thoughts and immediate responses to cultural stimuli, about capturing things floating in the digital air, a place to unleash insults and demonstrate a lack of consciousness—it was a machine *built* for outrage and skepticism. Yet did my Bigelow tweets *prove* that I was "truly demented"? Were they actually "sexist" and "toxic"? Was Kathryn Bigelow herself so important that calling her overrated—not incompetent or incapable—because she was beautiful had somehow crossed the line of decency?

The Bigelow tweets now crested with "I still believe that if 'The Hurt Locker' had been directed by a man it would not have won the Oscar for best director." I liked the definitiveness of this proclamation. It wasn't a searching tweet asking any kind of legitimate question—it was just another opinion, as well as a dig at reverse sexism—but my problem came with the reactions to the tweet: Why did people think I was *attacking her identity* instead of speculating about the fraudulence of the Oscars? Was this really going "too far," as some "followers" worried and alleged? Or was it just a fucking tweet? "Writer's SHOCKING Allegations!" read one protesting headline as if I'd just been accused of child molestation. The idea that some people thought I was becoming a "shit stirrer" was not only inaccurate but also failed to grasp the *context* of Twitter. Since you won't find "real life" on Twitter, none of this was supposed to be taken seriously, and I didn't care anyway that it was. I doubt that I've ever deleted a tweet.

■ ■ ■

But neither have I ever tweeted *at* anyone—as many people do—because to me that seemed too personal, too weirdly intimate, so maybe I never used Twitter the way others thought it was supposed to be used. I saw Twitter as more freewheeling and performative, and I rarely retweeted anyone. I didn't post links in case somebody wanted to find that interesting piece in *The London Review of Books* that I'd recommended or to the sites where you could purchase the novels I was rhapsodically banging on about (that prior fall it had been Paul Murray's *Skippy Dies*), and it was the same with bands and TV shows and movies or any other so-called content. I just tossed off thoughts, with no links or pics. My Twitter feed was opinionated, snarky, sometimes fake sincere, sometimes pissed-off, filled with reactions to good movies, bad movies, books I recommended, books I couldn't finish, quotations, occasionally just a song lyric from the past. These tweets appeared on my page randomly, in what I thought was the spirit of the site, at any given time of day, but mostly at night, sometimes after a few drinks, no questions, no explanations, just throwing out opinions and expressing myself to the lost souls who'd decided to follow me—though I was never genial in order to attract followers. I didn't try to be charming. My page either resonated or it didn't, and I had only vague ideas about why anyone would want to follow me at all. A few people suggested it was the "rancor" with which I expressed myself that prompted strangers to follow my verified account, and that I had "targets" they enjoyed seeing skewed, but this implied that my Twitter feed (and the very nature of the medium) was somehow *planned*. For me, it was, instead, something entirely spontaneous and random. But I did use Twitter to help a micro-budget movie I'd written get funded, as well as to find its male lead, and once to mistakenly, drunkenly, order drugs. I'd thought I was texting.

"Love is good, but hate is good, too," David Shields wrote in his manifesto *How Literature Saved My Life*, and in those early days that's how I used Twitter, enjoying the role of critic, whether by ridiculing the puffed-up pomposity of *The Newsroom* in its first month on HBO or pointing out that Michael Haneke's unceasingly brutal old-age love story *Amour* was what "*On Golden Pond* might have been like if it had been directed by Hitler." Twitter encouraged the bad boy in me, and I liked Twitter for that reason in 2012, tweeting at that time of night when all bets were off and the only things that seemed to matter for five minutes were the immediate responses my tweet received and that icy glass of tequila melting next to my keypad, throwing out stuff about Generation Wuss, the Gay Middlebrow, the legacy of David Foster Wallace, season five of *Mad Men*, the first season of *Girls*, how *Homeland* was so-so and why it's a really bad idea to have sex while you're watching *Game of Thrones*, about why I kept finding *Breaking Bad* so contrived, about Joan Didion's 1978 *Paris Review* interview, or just tweeting pics of my Christmas tree. Even if *The New York Times* had called my Twitter feed "brilliant" in the summer of 2013, I was always under attack, and it took me longer than it should have to understand why. Celebrity is an ephemeral game—it's totally different from being a writer, from the solitary work you do—and it makes you grow up fast, sometimes in hard ways. But if you've had a long career and already taken a lot of hits, you also realize after a while that they bounce off. You find out the armor was built so long ago that you assume everybody else on social media can handle the same bullets that you've been shot with—until you find out this is decisively untrue.

post-empire

In the summer of 2001 I was thirty-seven and my boyfriend had left New York for six months to study in Berlin. He was a decade younger than me, an artist who had addiction issues that we both assumed were under control until they weren't. I was solo that summer, left to my own devices—even though these ended up being somewhat less extravagant than what we shared as a hard-partying couple. But the summer was filled with a kind of low-humming dread, despite the supposed fun of promiscuity and drugs and relentless socializing. None of that could tamp down the dread that was hovering everywhere. It stemmed from the fact that earlier in the summer I'd been working out at the Crunch gym on Thirteenth Street, two blocks from my apartment, when I suddenly blacked out. When I regained consciousness I was in an ambulance that was taking me to St. Vincent's, accompanied by a trainer from the gym who told me at the hospital that I'd suffered a seizure, a pretty severe one. For some reason I decided that the seizure had to be connected to the upped dosages of Klonopin I was medicating myself with daily to take the edge off, and the dehydration that probably afflicted me because of the very-hard-drinking crew I hung out with; add to that the hellish heat in the city that summer, as well as the weird bouts of insomnia I was fighting: to me all this seemed the perfect recipe for that seizure.

Yet maybe it was caused by something else, so I started getting fearful, and in the packed waiting room at St. Vincent's, flat on a stretcher, I began to panic and was convinced something black and awful would engulf me along with everybody else in that packed waiting room if I didn't get out of St. Vincent's immediately. I left the waiting room, the trainer from Crunch trailing behind and trying to persuade me to stay until I was standing on a corner of Seventh Avenue trying to wave down a cab, my arm lightly bleeding from an injection, my legs wobbling, a headache blinding everything.

My doctor, whose offices were in the Zeckendorf Towers just a block up from my apartment, had been informed about the seizure and wanted to run some tests because to him it didn't sound like the kind of seizure that was caused by a mild addiction to a benzodiazepine mixed with dehydration and alcohol. I kept promising to come in but the fear of him finding something stopped those tests from happening, and so a summer continued where I was unable to concentrate on the novel I'd been working on and the number of guys I was juggling seemed mystifying since I'd never been promiscuous, and there was the cocaine, and there was the insomnia, which had nothing to do with the cocaine. And then there was the stalker who had invaded the narrative somewhere in that summer as well.

■ ■ ■

Long handwritten fan letters were being sent directly to me at the apartment on Thirteenth Street, instead of to my publishing house or my agent's office, and that fact alone was, during this particular summer, alarming enough. But it was the content of the letters that heightened my dread even further: demands for me to get back to this person, an insistence that we belonged *together*, that this person knew with a certainty that I was truly *the only one*, and if anyone else had me there was the not-so-obscure indication that they eventually wouldn't be able to have me—the meaning of this filled with a tangible threat. The letters kept coming with no return address, just a PO box, and soon packages started arriving filled with "gifts," including a variety of "spices" in small plastic bags that my admirer wanted me to mix into liquids so I could drink them and get on the same "wavelength"—and then came the letter intimating that my admirer and I should ingest a deadly mix of powders together, which would allow us to have sex in heaven and experience "multitudes of orgasms." By now I'd realized the admirer was watching my building, knew when I was home, followed my progression throughout the city and, at one point, got past the front desk while the doormen were trading shifts and tried to get into my apartment. Add this to the seizure, the drugs, the heat, the insomnia, the repeated phone calls from my doctor urging me to make an appointment, the absent partner in Berlin, the book on which I was now blocked—it all blew up.

Today, I would have addressed all of these problems like an adult, but for some reason at thirty-seven the fear exploded childishly, and I remember very clearly on an August afternoon finding myself on the phone with the security division of the ICM literary agency—I didn't know they even *had* a security division—as they asked me a series of routine questions about my "stalker" in a soothing tone while I paced the apartment. The security team had asked me to place everything I had received from the stalker into individual plastic bags, which had already been picked up, and the head of security was now looking at them while he was on the phone with me that August afternoon. The bemused tone of his voice as he asked the perfunctory questions both calmed and enraged me. *You're not taking this seriously,* I wanted to scream. *This person's ruining my life.* But in that same moment I was thinking this, another voice in the back of my head was whispering, *No,* you're *ruining your life.* And suddenly that day I found a new and more coherent beginning for the novel I'd been having trouble writing. This was when the real story of *Lunar Park* began to change and reshape itself: the writer creating the more convenient and more dramatic narrative over the cold and less dramatic neutrality of facts became, in a way, the metaphor of this book, and of how his misinterpretation could lead to chaos and horror.

The stalker, my admirer, was in fact just an overly determined fan, and a week later the man from the security division filled me in on how they'd located this elusive person who both craved contact and yet had been linked only to her PO box address—yes, it was a woman—and the voice over the phone told me they had "dealt" with her and, when I asked what that meant, exactly, the voice over the phone told me not to worry about it anymore: she wouldn't make contact again. And she didn't. This was sometime in late August, and it prompted me to take a series of tests to determine what might or might not have caused the seizure. I cut back on the cocaine, cut back mildly on the drinking, started backing away from the random guys, drafted a new outline for *Lunar Park* and began writing with a fervor that just hadn't existed during the two years since I'd initiated the project. I started sleeping through the night uninterrupted. Things were clearing up. The haze was lifting.

■ ■ ■

On the night of September 10 I excused myself early from a party in Lower Manhattan that I'd attended with the writer Jonathan Lethem, and where I would have lingered if I didn't have a doctor's appointment—a kind of final checkup—early the next morning. I had an 8:30 appointment at the Zeckendorf—nothing had been found, the cause of the seizure was never located—and as I sat in my doctor's office being examined one last time a nurse walked in, handed him something, and mentioned that a small plane had hit the World Trade Center—yes, people who weren't in the vicinity thought, at first, it was a *small* plane—and the doctor and I thought this was curious and maybe cracked a nervous joke but then the nurse walked in again and said another plane had hit the other tower. A faint, swirling panic set in as we left the examining room and went into the waiting room, where everyone stood below a wall-mounted television and watched the smoke billowing out of the towers, all of us transfixed with confusion and clearly aware that something was deeply wrong. I quickly left the Zeckendorf and walked the two blocks back to the apartment on Thirteenth Street and I'll never forget how crystal clear, how insanely blue the sky was that morning above the trees in Union Square Park. In my apartment I watched the towers collapse on TV while talking on the phone with my mother, who had called from Los Angeles until we were cut off. I felt, for one of the only times in my life, a real and uncontrollable fear that day, a kind of freezing terror that anything could happen, anything was permissible, that what happened this morning opened up a new door altogether, and that everything was out of control. It also felt like the culmination of everything I had experienced during the summer of 2001.

I remember only two things from that day. A girl came over to my apartment before noon, hysterical: friends of hers had escaped the towers early on and she was telling me about one in particular who had gotten out and was stepping onto the street when he was suddenly sprayed in the face with warm water. He had no idea where this water had come from and then it rapidly happened again, dousing his face and the suit he was wearing until he realized almost instantly that it wasn't water at all but had come from a falling body that had hit a nearby lamppost. I haven't been able to shake off this detail since I first heard it, nor the images I connected with it: the young man walking home covered in blood to his apartment in the West Village and collapsing on the floor of his shower sobbing as he scrubbed the blood off. The other thing I remember clearly is walking around the East Village that night in a daze, picking up takeout Thai food on Second Avenue and seeing two wasted girls at the bar of the restaurant, both of them laughing drunkenly, a sound I've never forgotten because it almost seemed like a small act of defiance, a rebuke, even if it wasn't, and I was honestly relieved to hear it. *This is the world we now live in,* a voice in my mind kept hissing as I made my way back to the apartment.

■ ■ ■

The next three days there was nowhere to go, nothing to do: we just watched TV. The entire city was swallowed up by the tragedy and you could literally smell it in the air if you lived in Manhattan, a kind of chemical reek that took weeks to dissipate. That first week everything happened with a stunned deliberation and there was nothing else to reference except this disaster, this apocalypse. And yet, because of it I took refuge in the book I'd to this point been stuck on and now began moving forward with a certainty and clarity that was not only a needed distraction but also genuinely exciting—and in the following weeks a new appetite was unleashed: I wanted to write in a way I never had before, and admittedly haven't since. I remember feeling this so distinctly after the initial horror wore off—a rising toward something, an optimism. I wasn't going to complain anymore. I would no longer be scared. I'd get things done. This sounded spiritually mundane but it was *real.* The first book I picked up after 9/11 was *The Corrections,* and found myself so immersed in it that I was often as grateful it simply existed in this moment as I was moved by the narrative itself and also deeply relieved that I was able to concentrate on reading a novel again. But reminders of what had happened would always be with us it seemed. That autumn, a group of us had dinner one night in Tribeca and then moved aimlessly down to Ground Zero, in our suits and dresses, buzzed and chattering, somehow slipping past each subsequent barricade until we were actually standing at the site itself; it had been cleaned up by then, there was nothing there, and it was brightly lit as if on display, the white sodium lights revealing what had once existed now swept away, and what moved us into silence was how small it looked.

■ ■ ■

All of this came back to me a few years ago, in 2015, while I was watching Alex Gibney's epic 248-minute HBO documentary about Frank Sinatra, *All or Nothing at All.* I found myself thinking about Empire, the American culture I'd grown up with, and once more I was reminded of, and overwhelmed by, how much cultural power Sinatra had amassed and consolidated for himself as a pop performer at the height of Empire in mid-twentieth-century America. I'd thought I knew the Sinatra story pretty well, but Gibney fills in the major events with a tidal wave of archival footage that I'd never seen before, and the effect is so hypnotic that although I thought I was only going to watch the first two hours on that Monday night in April, I changed my mind. Part one ended with Sinatra's comeback in 1953, and I was wiped out not only by the intensity of Gibney's approach, but also by Sinatra's tenacity, so I spent the rest of the evening watching the second part, completely rapt at the exhilarating ride that constituted the rest of the Sinatra story as it unfolded for another two hours: the big years, the great records, Vegas, a pop performer whose life mirrored the century in which he came of age—Sinatra's trajectory was America's trajectory. He was a self-made king and the first modern pop star, complete with thousands of screaming teenage girls mobbing his early performances—a phenomenon that hadn't happened before. But Sinatra's story is really about pragmatism, defeat, loss, pain and the romantic disappointment that (in the guise of Ava Gardner) nearly destroyed him, and about the way he turned these things, those feelings and that hurt, into *art*, deepening the songs he was simply performing (he didn't write any of them). Through the force of his artistry, he both caught and created the mood of a nation and connected with a massive audience that is unthinkable now. I'm not talking about racking up a billion YouTube hits, but about an entire country that was lastingly stirred.

The Gibney film skirts some big stories, among them the death of Sinatra's mother and the Hollywood movies he made in the 1960s and into the '70s, and you're sometimes reminded that the documentary was created with the approval of his estate. At times it seems we're witnessing a settling of scores, especially when the film explains Sinatra's disillusionment with John F. Kennedy after he'd campaigned for him incessantly and was then shut out of the White House because of the same mob ties that Sinatra had called on to help Kennedy win the election. But *All or Nothing at All* stays on its point that Sinatra was an artist, with pain and regret and loss informing his greatest work, and though he wasn't a songwriter, he rewrote the songs he sang with his phrasing and vocal inflections and with a doomy pragmatism that permeated everything from "That's Life" to "Summer Wind" to "It Was a Very Good Year." Sinatra was also open in interviews and joked around drunkenly onstage with the Rat Pack: an Empire performer who *believed* in the power of Empire. How could he not? It built him. He influenced it. Sinatra seemingly said and did whatever he wanted. Free and white and male, he could be loose and funny, contradictory at times, outspoken and playful, sometimes a bully, or else lost or haunted, glamorous, argumentative, even plain *weird*—just a man, unapologetically.

Sinatra never apologized for anything because that kind of culture didn't exist then—a world where anyone, even prominent people, could be policed into muteness—although he was occasionally attacked by the press about his appetite for women and the louche Rat Pack years in Las Vegas, which he single-handedly reinvented as a mecca for tourists. He knew everyone, a vast and amazing cast that stretched from Hollywood to New York to Washington, D.C. Sinatra somewhat foundered in the late '60s, unable to figure out where he stood when surrounded by the Beatles and the Doors, and when he retired in 1971, people thought it was the right time in a rock era where he came off as vaguely fossilized. Yet in typical Sinatra fashion, his restlessness moved him to stage a comeback tour in 1974, and he continued to perform in sold-out stadiums—the crowds got bigger—until his death in 1998.

Watching *All or Nothing at All,* I was reminded there can never be another Sinatra because neither pop culture nor our society works like that anymore—in a way that allows someone to fail repeatedly and to get back up, to act brashly, and sometimes badly, without apology. Pop culture now would be hesitant to invite anyone like Sinatra (or Miles Davis or James Brown) back in, and while watching Gibney's movie it chilled me to realize that maybe this democratization hadn't been all that great for pop culture itself. How would any of those artists have fared in a self-censorious society in which everyone tiptoes around trying to appease every group that might take offense at any opposing view, in essence shutting down creative excellence thanks to the fears and insecurities and ignorance of others? Could Sinatra have been forced into singing songs that exclusively made us feel dreamily better about our own *identities*, while ignoring the painful realities of life and human existence? And as the movie ended, I hated thinking what might've happened to Sinatra in a day and age when, for example, he sang "the lady is a tramp" in a song? *Misogyny!* A chief of the white male patriarchy! Toxic masculinity! Don't buy his records, comrade! Boycott the label! Sinatra would have been disgusted by the Orwellian tenor of our current moment, but I can't imagine he would have ever bowed to it.

■ ■ ■

"*Drugs?*" is the first word Charlie Sheen utters in his only scene from *Ferris Bueller's Day Off*, a Reagan-era epic from the summer of 1986 whose ad line was "Leisure Rules" and is the one John Hughes teen movie that seems the least dated. This four-minute scene, expertly written and directed, takes place in a police station in suburban Chicago where uptight Jeannie Bueller (Jennifer Grey), waiting to get bailed out by her mom and fuming about brother Ferris's charmingly anarchic ways (he breaks all the rules and is happy; she follows all the rules and is unhappy), realizes she's sitting next to a gorgeous sullen-eyed dude in a leather jacket who looks like he's been up for days on a drug binge, but he's not manic, just tired and sexily calm, his face so pale it's almost violet-hued. "Drugs?" is the first thing he asks Jeannie. Annoyed, Jeannie asks, "Why are *you* here?" and Sheen answers, deadpan and with no regret, now referring to himself: "Drugs." And then he slowly disarms her bitchiness with an outrageously sexy insouciance, transforming her annoyance into delight—and they end up making out.

This hypnotic scene near the end of *Ferris Bueller's Day Off* is when a few of us first really noticed Charlie Sheen, and it remains a key moment in his movie career, and it now seems to define and sum up everything that followed. Looking over his filmography, he was never again quite as magnetic until the breakdown he had in the winter of 2011, when he finally got fired from his starring role in the massively successful sitcom *Two and a Half Men*. Sheen grew up in 1970s Malibu and was expelled from Santa Monica High and he was never a trained actor—he just kicked around in a few underwhelming movies before starring within the space of a year in two key Empire films, both directed by Oliver Stone: *Platoon* (1986) and *Wall Street* (1987). Sheen was never considered a good actor, but he pulled off the "Who am I?" line as Bud Fox with just the right note of yuppie bewilderment, and the camera liked him. Yet even as he starred in the comedies and spoofs that followed he seemed wooden, more a good sport than a natural clown; he had too much pride to really cut loose on-screen. But he became TV's highest-paid actor with *Two and a Half Men*, until the trauma of 2011, when he began to respond to his celebrity in the post-Empire world. This new world was all about personal transparency, just as the Empire world that had created and heralded Sheen was about masks and propriety, being an actor. Yet he abruptly shrugged off the secret burdens of Empire celebrity and in doing so, freed himself.

■ ■ ■

The horror of 9/11 represented the end of Empire, a shock that moved us out of the twentieth century's binary Cold War thinking (*The center will not hold*) and into a world where there was, and is, no center; our enemies are insurgent and decentralized, our media also decentralized and insurgent. The culture seemed like it no longer belonged to the titans but instead to whoever could seize its attention with whatever immediacy and force. If Empire was about the heroic American figure—solid, rooted in tradition, tactile and analog—then post-Empire was about people who were understood to be ephemeral right away; digital disposability doesn't concern them—they're rooted in traditions created by social media, which is solely about exhibition and surface, and they don't follow a now dated path of artistic and cultural development. They're about hypnotizing our attention for only as long as their loud bid can last, which is why they don't adhere to conventional media pieties.

America as it existed at the height of Empire began to reveal itself in the prosperous postwar 1950s, defining and expressing itself through the rise of the mass mediums of television, movies and pop music, of celebrity itself, and it ran roughly through 9/11. Empire limped along through the rest of the Bush presidency, at least until the economy blew up, and then Obama was elected, social media grew dominant, and programming shifted to accommodate the new cultural needs that formed after this cataclysm. If Empire was the Eagles, Veuve Clicquot, Reagan, *The Godfather* and Robert Redford, then post-Empire was *American Idol*, coconut water, the Tea Party, *The Human Centipede*, and Shia LaBeouf. With expectations diminished everywhere there was a shrugging off of Establishment propriety, a refusal to bow to a system that wasn't working, and outsider attitudes were pushed into the mainstream—attitudes marked by a lack of polish, a do-it yourself mind-set, an impulse to carelessly wear your pajamas in public. It was a brief moment that never fully flowered; it existed fleetingly and then, like everything else, became watered down and clamped shut, as the post-Empire merged into corporate culture. Yet post-Empire hasn't entirely disappeared. Traces remain everywhere, and certainly Donald Trump is a post-Empire president, while the legacy media's reaction to him has never seemed more reactionary and belongs to full-blown Empire.

■ ■ ■

Post-Empire attained the mainstream in 2010 and 2011 with Cee Lo Green's "Fuck You" gleefully providing the soundtrack and examples began flourishing everywhere. The Kardashians understood it, as did MTV's *Jersey Shore*'s participants and audience. We saw it when Lady Gaga arrived at the Grammys that year sealed in an egg and stared down Anderson Cooper in a *60 Minutes* segment, admitting she liked to smoke weed when writing songs and basically daring him, "What are you going to do about *that*, bitch?" Nicki Minaj grasped it when she assumed one of her various bizarre alter-egos on the red carpet, and yet Christina Aguilera didn't get it at all when starring in *Burlesque*, while continuing to ape Empire attitudes by idolizing and glamorizing herself unironically. Ricky Gervais, freewheeling and insulting as he hosted the Golden Globes in January 2011, understood, while Robert Downey Jr., getting passive-aggressively pissed-off at Gervais during the same show, didn't seem to, and Robert De Niro, subtly ridiculing his career while accepting his lifetime achievement award, generally understood it as well—though later, in lamely attacking Trump, he seemed like an unhinged old-school poser.

John Mayer at one point looked like he was going to be the original post-Empire poster boy for his TMZ appearances (he was the first celebrity to realize what a game changer TMZ would be) and also provided a key example of post-Empire in his racially and sexually charged *Playboy* interview in 2010, until he apologized for it. Kanye West scored a major post-Empire moment with his interruption of Taylor Swift's acceptance speech at the 2009 Video Music Awards, as well as with his masterpiece post-Empire single "Runaway"—whereas Bruno Mars or Bono, not so much. James Franco, hosting that year's Oscar telecast without taking it seriously, treating it with gentle disrespect, gave another instance of post-Empire performance, while his peppy and earnest cohost, Anne Hathaway, didn't appear to have a clue. Post-Empire was Mark Zuckerberg staring with blank impatience at Leslie Stahl on *60 Minutes* when telling her how *The Social Network* got its genesis story totally wrong—by suggesting he'd created Facebook because he was rejected by a bitchy girl—and that this conceit had been dreamt up by the Empire screenwriter Aaron Sorkin. For every outspoken I-don't-give-a-fuck Empire celebrity—whether Muhammad Ali or Gore Vidal or Bob Dylan or John Lennon or even Joni Mitchell—there were always dozens like Madonna, a true queen of Empire, who never seemed real or funny, everything about her looking, in retrospect, dreadfully earnest and manufactured, or Michael Jackson, the ultimate victim of Empire celebrity, a tortured boy lover and drug addict who humorlessly denied he was either. Keith Richards, in his 2010 memoir *Life*, was a rare example of a healthy, post-Empire geezer transparency, and for my younger friends this kind of transparency was increasingly the norm: What did shame mean anymore?

In 2011, post-Empire wasn't just about publicly admitting doing "illicit" things and coming clean; it was a then-radical attitude that claimed the Empire lie no longer existed—realness, transparency, and the tactility of your flesh were the only qualities that mattered. To the former gatekeepers, someone like Charlie Sheen seemed dangerous and in need of help because he was destroying illusions about the nature of Empire celebrity—as did Trump five years later. Sheen had long been a role model for a certain kind of male fantasy, a degrading one, perhaps, but isn't that true of most male fantasies? (I never knew any straight men who fantasized about Tom Cruise's personal life.) Sheen had always been a bad boy, which was part of his appeal for men *and* women, and this was what Chuck Lorre, the co-creator of *Two and a Half Men*, initially responded to—a manly mock dignity that both sexes liked a lot. What Sheen exemplified and clarified was that not giving a fuck about what the public thinks about you or your personal life is actually what matters the most, that the public will respond to you even more fervently, because you're free and that's exactly what they all desire—everyone, that is, except for the network or the show's creator or the corporation that has made you so fabulously wealthy.

■ ■ ■

Post-Empire narcissism differed greatly from Empire narcissism. Eminem was post-Empire's most outspoken mainstream character when he first appeared in the late '90s, and we suddenly were light-years away from the autobiographical pain of, say, Dylan's *Blood on the Tracks*, one of Empire's proudest and most stylish achievements. It wasn't as if craft wasn't the point anymore, only that a different sort of self-expression was in play—less diluted, more raw, immediate, and prone to anxiety and fear and weakness. On *The Marshall Mathers LP* Eminem raged much more transparently than Dylan had against the idiocy of his own flaws and the failure of *his* marriage, as well as about his addictions and fantasies—maybe even more than any Empire artist ever had—and he fearlessly recorded the imagined murder of his ex-wife by his own enraged hands, a defiant act that Bob Dylan or Bruce Springsteen would never have even contemplated. *Blood on the Tracks* and *Tunnel of Love* had an Empire tastefulness and boomer elegance that in the post-Empire world—digital and disposable and DIY—had no meaning. This didn't deny Dylan or Springsteen their power or artistry, it simply reflected that people no longer cared as much about these things.

Extolling celebrity in a time when it had never seemed more fleeting or ephemeral meant a lot more people became famous for doing nothing of much interest. In HBO's 2010 documentary—produced by Graydon Carter and directed by Martin Scorsese, pranksters who became heavyweight champions of Empire—Fran Lebowitz complained that what had really been lost in American culture was connoisseurship: the ability for someone to recognize the difference between what was genuinely good and what was merely mediocre. She bemoaned the fact that we didn't seem to be at a point anymore when being extremely good at something—and getting rewarded for that talent with attention, respect and money—was even regarded as *possible*. That era wasn't really gone in 2011, at least not in Lebowitz's alarmist perspective, yet every day in American culture it *felt* as if it might have evaporated, but, again, only if you had an Empire viewpoint. Very few people were becoming famous because they could actually *do* interesting things, and Charlie Sheen, admittedly, was not one of them. He staggered amiably through a bad sitcom—Sheen was fine, he was inoffensive, he barely engaged with anyone on the show and retained a semi-stunned look of disgust at the shoddiness and smarminess of the proceedings. If he'd been allowed to give Charlie Harper more personality—a spark, a genuine leer—this probably would've thrown the sitcom woodenness of *Two and a Half Men* off-balance.

The contempt for the material that Sheen voiced during his breakdown made the show briefly more interesting than it had ever been, but never enough to warrant enduring an entire episode. He had publicly denounced *Two and a Half Men* as "comfort TV" and a "tin can" of a show that was "a puke fest that everybody watches," but did its fans actually care or were they really bothered if the star criticized his own show or snorted cocaine and bought hookers and allegedly abused women? Every time there was a lapse in Charlie Sheen's imaginary morals clause (he didn't, in fact, have one) the series ratings reliably bumped up. For Sheen to trudge through a sitcom he knew was awful in order to make the big bucks ($1.8 million per episode) had to itself be a kind of princely nightmare. It wasn't as if he was playing Don Draper, or even Jack Donaghy from *30 Rock*. He was playing an unamusing and watered-down version of Charlie Sheen, and that must have sucked. Performing those scenes and delivering those one-liners week after week after week probably would have sent anyone racing off for drugs and alcohol and hookers, and one might have expected the people who'd hired and rehired him, and who understood he'd helped make them an enormous amount of money, to simply ignore his weekend escapades and let the cameras roll when he showed up for work on Monday morning. But later, in that winter of 2011, Sheen no longer had to bear this onerous responsibility, since he got fired.

■ ■ ■

During the fall of 2010, his *Two and a Half Men* costar Jon Cryer had noted that in the beginning of the eighth season Sheen had arrived on set gaunt and pale, sallow and sweaty; his timing was off, and he was rushing lines if he could remember them at all. After Sheen refused to talk to executives concerned about his behavior—when he refused to play that game—he walked off the show to complete an at-home drug rehab, his third attempt to get clean in a year. During this time-out, he publicly made derogatory comments about Chuck Lorre and demanded a raise that would have upped his episode price to $2.7 million, which Sheen said would still be an underpayment compared to what Lorre, Warner Bros., and CBS were making from the show. He also suggested that he was a "warlock" with "tiger blood" and "Adonis DNA." People were missing the point if they thought Charlie Sheen's breakdown was only a story about drugs. They definitely played their part but were not at the core of what was happening or what made the flameout in the winter of 2011 so fascinating to the public. Functioning addicts aren't that rare or interesting since everybody knows one or two, but Sheen's reaction to it seemed like the crystallization of post-Empire conduct. This wasn't about the wives, or his five kids, or even the HIV diagnosis he received during that period, a catalyst Sheen later blamed for his misbehavior (and he'd paid extortionists $10 million to keep quiet until his diagnosis was revealed by the media in 2015). This was about Sheen himself, the man who no longer could attempt his real life while working as an actor, a profoundly dismayed *individual.* The narrative that unfolded featured a well-earned midlife crisis that was playing out on CNN instead of in a life coach's office somewhere in Burbank: the midlife crisis being the moment in a man's life when he realizes he can't—that he won't—maintain the pose he'd thought was required of him for a single day longer.

■ ■ ■

Tom Cruise had a similar meltdown at the same age in the summer of 2005, but his had been more politely manufactured and, of course, Cruise was never known as an addict. Cruise had his breakdown while trying to smile through gritted teeth, and he couldn't get loose—there was a refusal to be up-front about it. This was a reminder that he had always been a good kid who couldn't say "Fuck you" as adroitly as Sheen could; Cruise was still the altar boy from Syracuse who earnestly believed in the glamour of Empire. This was ultimately a limitation for him as a movie star and as an actor heading into post-Empire—it seemed like he was hiding something all the time, which might explain why he was so explosive in *Magnolia* as the liar who gets caught. Tact might have worked for Cruise in the days of Empire, but something like *Knight and Day* just didn't fly in the new world. And Les Grossman, the monstrous, foul-mouthed studio executive from *Tropic Thunder*, gyrating on the MTV Movie Awards, wasn't Cruise getting post-Empire loose because Les Grossman tapped into a giant part of how Cruise actually came off in the mainstream press—Empire control freakery at its most clenched. This was why some people thought Les Grossman was funny: because the character seemed to parody a side of Cruise that was recognizable. Cruise was a prince of the Empire and not even playing Les Grossman, swearing and in a fat suit, was going to erase that—even though it was the right idea. Sheen was a minor member of the Empire by comparison, so it was surprising that *he* became the star who solidified and paid the price for this transitional phase of post-Empire celebrity.

■ ■ ■

What was another Les—Les Moonves, the CEO of CBS—thinking about Charlie Sheen during those travails in 2011? On one level he must have tolerated, if not exactly approved of, some of what took place years before the official firing: the arrests and the accidental overdose in which Sheen suffered a stroke after injecting cocaine; the half-hearted stints in rehab and his father Martin's teary-eyed press conference; the briefcase full of coke and the Mercedes towed out of the ravine; the misdemeanor third-degree assault on his third wife, who also ended up entering rehab for crack addiction, and Sheen's alleged threat to cut off her head, put it in a box and *send it to her mother*; or, later, Sheen's appearance on TMZ, chain-smoking and gesturing to the twenty-four-year-old "goddesses" he was now shacking up with, in which he appeared alternately bored and enjoying himself while he railed against CBS and Warner Bros., who had, by that point, decided to cancel the rest of *Two and a Half Men*'s eighth season and later that week, fire him. (Of CBS executives he had remarked, "They lay down with their ugly wives in front of their ugly children and look at their loser lives.") What about the September 11 conspiracy theories Sheen believed in and the fact he was a member of the 9/11 Truth Movement, or that he'd fucked Ginger Lynn and Heather Hunter and Bree Olson, had shot Kelly Preston in the arm and been a regular client of Heidi Fleiss, the Hollywood Madam? What about him trashing a Manhattan hotel room, with a porn star locked in the bathroom while his wife Denise Richards and the kids were sleeping across the hall; or his refusal to admit that he'd hit rock bottom—"a fishing term," Sheen scoffed—or claiming that his PR person had lied about the "medication mix-up?" Yet, up until the fateful eighth season, he had always managed to show up for work and hadn't damaged *Two and a Half Men*'s reputation despite all the drugs and whoring. But in the aftermath, Sheen began putting on a mesmerizing and refreshing display of midlife-crisis honesty. He was only being himself, take it or leave it, an addict and an actor who just didn't want to act anymore.

Sheen was all over the media landscape in the winter of 2011—on the new Piers Morgan show on CNN, on *20/20* and TMZ, and he never seemed like he was on drugs, whether he was or not. The uncut TMZ interview was a post-Empire triumph, and he looked great talking to Piers Morgan, who after an uneven inaugural month seemed finally, happily excited with Sheen's aggressive transparency—try sitting through Morgan's interview with Empire diva Janet Jackson, which was filled with so many evasive pauses you could have rolled boulders through them. And for the first time in his thirty-year career, Sheen himself seemed a genuinely interesting person—maybe a wreck and a mess, but *real* and as flawed and fucked-up as any of us. Transparency was now Sheen's thing in that moment, and it was thrilling to watch someone call out the solemnity of the celebrity interview for the sham that it was. He was raw and lucid and intense and he was suddenly the most fascinating celebrity wandering through the culture. No one was used to these kinds of interviews because no one had ever seen anything like them—they almost approached performance art—because Sheen wasn't apologizing for anything.

■ ■ ■

Charlie Sheen had severe drug and alcohol problems, and perhaps even struggled with mental illness, but so did a lot of people in Hollywood who simply were better at hiding it. There was no denying that Sheen was exploiting a problematic situation that he'd helped create, but you couldn't ignore the fact that the negativity certain people felt about him never outweighed the public's fascination with the hedonism he clearly enjoyed and that remained the secret envy of many other men. Sheen's supposed propensity for violence against women hadn't hurt his popularity with female fans either, and if anyone wants to know what *that* means, then that's a story for maybe fifty *other* books. It now appeared that the manners and civility and courtesy that Empire had demanded and enforced had ceased to exist. And that what the new guard wanted above all was *reality*, no matter how crazy the celeb who'd brought it on actually was. This was what enflamed corporations like CBS and the legacy media and the entertainment press but also gave them boners even as they were wringing their hands and clutching their pearls.

Charlie Sheen apparently didn't care what they thought about him anymore, and he ridiculed public relations taboos and the cult of likability. *Hey suits, hey corporations, I don't give a shit—you all suck* was what so many of the disenfranchised were responding to in the winter of 2011. Sheen was blowing open the myth that men would outgrow the adolescent pursuit of pleasure, because flickers of that dream would never go out. Even if you were married and had terrific kids, the dream of living without fake rules and responsibilities, of rejecting the notion of becoming an ideal, a clean and spotless comrade enthralled by groupthink, the dream of being an *individual* and not just part of some tribe would always survive. Charlie Sheen was the new reality, and anyone who was a hater now had to hang out with the rest of the collective in Empire's graveyard. Nobody had known it in the summer of 1986, but Charlie Sheen had actually been Ferris Bueller's dark little brother all along.

■ ■ ■

In the decades after it was published, readers of *American Psycho* often asked me where Patrick Bateman would be now, as if he were an acquaintance of mine, someone real I used to know. This often came up during the tech boom of the mid-'90s, and after the movie version was released in 2000, and again post-9/11 and during the Bush presidency, and it came up urgently in the months after the 2008 housing crash, and the question became even more prevalent on the twenty-fifth anniversary of its publication in 2016, which happened to coincide with a Broadway musical based on the book that was opening that spring, and it was never posed more desperately than it was after Donald Trump was elected.

This question was asked because of how specific the setting of *American Psycho* is, and it was asked by fans at readings and signings or on social media, and by colleagues at pitch meetings or on conference calls, sometimes as an icebreaker, and it was asked whenever guys posted pictures of Halloween costumes—in which they were wearing the sheer blood-splattered slicker that Christian Bale's Bateman sported in the film version when he killed his Pierce & Pierce rival Paul Allen (Jared Leto) with an ax to the face. In particular, they wondered where the Wall Street yuppie and supposed serial killer who'd haunted the late-'80s streets and nightclubs and restaurants of Manhattan would be if he were re-created and resituated, if he were actually alive, tactile, wandering through our world in flesh and blood.

If you'd read the book carefully and had a sense of Manhattan geography, you knew that Bateman's sleek and minimalist Upper West Side apartment had an imaginary address, and this always suggested to me that Bateman wasn't necessarily a reliable narrator, and that he might in fact be a ghost, an idea, a summing up of that particular decade's values as filtered through my own literary sensibility: moneyed, beautifully attired, impossibly groomed and handsome, morally bankrupt, totally isolated and filled with rage, a young and directionless mannequin hoping that someone, anyone, will save him from himself.

■ ■ ■

During the mid- to late '90s—at the height of the dotcom bubble, when Manhattan seemed even more absurdly decadent than it did in 1987—it was a possibility that Bateman, if the book had been moved a decade closer, might have been the founder of several dotcoms, and that he would've partied in Tribeca and the Hamptons, indistinguishable from the young and handsome boy wonders who were commanding the scene with their millions of nonexistent dollars, dancing unknowingly on the edge of an implosion that would mercilessly wipe out the playing field and correct all sorts of bogus scores. While twirling through that decade myself as a youngish man, I often thought this was a time in which Bateman really could've thrived, especially with the advent of new technologies that would have aided his ghoulish obsession with torture and murder and offered him new methods of recording them. And sometimes I thought that if I'd set the book in the 2000s Bateman could've been working in Silicon Valley, living in Cupertino with excursions into San Francisco or down to Big Sur to the Post Ranch Inn, palling around with Zuckerberg and dining at the French Laundry or lunching with Reed Hastings at Manresa in Los Gatos, wearing a Yeezy hoodie and teasing girls on Tinder. He could also just as easily have been a hedge funder in New York: Patrick Bateman begets Bill Ackman and Daniel Loeb.

In 2002, two years after the original movie had opened theatrically, there was a shoddy, barely released sequel called *American Psycho II: All American Girl* that had little to do with Patrick Bateman, who's killed off in the first five minutes. The film was adapted from a script titled *The Girl Who Wouldn't Die*, which was originally conceived as a thriller with no connection whatsoever to my book, and it wasn't until production began that the script was altered by Lionsgate to incorporate a Bateman subplot, because of the success the studio had with producing *American*

Psycho. There was also talk at Lionsgate about a TV series that would either continue the Bateman saga or update it to the present day. Patrick Bateman action figures were being sold online, and then came *American Psycho: The Musical*, which after a sold-out London run in 2013 was transferred to Broadway in March 2016. All of this encouraged me to wonder not only about where Bateman might have been then in these various moments in time, but also about how this character was created in the first place.

How strange it was to see the embodiment of my youthful pain and angst morph into a metaphor for the disruptive greed of an entire decade, as well as a continuing metaphor for people who work on Wall Street—an abiding symbol of corruption—or for anyone whose perfect façade masks a wilder, dirtier side, as in: "My boyfriend's *such* a Patrick Bateman." As the book's author I still have no idea why—and I can't take any responsibility for this—it had such resonance, though it might be that the moment we were living in then was, if anything, even riper for the metaphor of a serial killer, a ripeness that has extended far beyond that into a Donald Trump presidency. Part of why it was hard for me to reimagine Bateman anywhere else or at any other time was because of where I was emotionally and physically during those years I was dreaming him up, so I've never had an answer for anyone who asked me.

■ ■ ■

I find it stranger as I get older that this archetypal character—for me more or less a faceless and free-floating representation of yuppie despair—was actually based on my own anger and frustration, in a very specific time and place. Moving to Manhattan after graduating from college with a BA—a phrase seemingly embalmed in some distant era, such an antiquated fantasy at a time when grads can't afford to even *think* about moving to Manhattan—I found myself in a world that had swallowed the values of the Reagan '80s as a kind of hope, an aspiration, something to rise toward. I disagreed with the ideology that was being so widely embraced but I was still trying, as Bateman puts it, to fit in. While I might have been turned off by such gross ambitions—and by what they suggested it meant to be a man, much less a successful one—where else was there to go? (True, I'd already published two novels, but they had nothing to do with the emptiness I was now feeling.) Doesn't the whole process of becoming an adult start with learning how to navigate these waters, even compromising one's youthful ideals and learning how to be all right with wherever you ended up? The rage I felt over what was being extolled as *success*—what seemed expected of me and other male members of Gen X, including millions of dollars, six-pack abs, and a cold amorality—was poured directly into a fictional figure who was my own worst version of myself, the nightmarish me, someone I loathed but also considered, in his helpless floundering, sympathetic as often as not. And his social criticism sounded to me almost entirely correct.

American Psycho was about what it meant to be a person in a society you disagreed with and what happened when you attempted to accept and live with its values even if you knew they were wrong. Delusion and anxiety were the focal points. Insanity crept in and was overwhelming. This was the outcome of chasing the American dream: isolation, alienation, corruption, the consumerist void in thrall to technology and corporate culture. All of the novel's themes still hold sway three decades later when the one-percenters were suddenly richer than any humans had ever been before, an era when a jet was as commonplace as a new car and million-dollar rents were a reality. New York in 2016 and beyond was *American Psycho* on steroids. And despite the connections provided by the internet and social media, many people felt even more isolated and increasingly aware that the idea of interconnectivity was itself an illusion. This seems particularly painful when you're sitting alone in a room and staring at a glowing screen that promises you access to the intimacies of countless other lives, a condition that mirrors Bateman's loneliness and alienation: everything's available to him, yet that insatiable emptiness remains. These were my own feelings during those years in the apartment I was living in on East Thirteenth Street as the 1980s came to an end.

In the period when the novel takes place, Patrick Bateman already belongs to the as-yet-unnamed one percent, as he probably still would today. But would he be living somewhere else, and with different interests? Would better forensics—not to mention the Big Brother cameras on virtually every corner—prevent him from getting away with the murders he at least tells the reader he has committed, or would his expression of rage take any other form? Would he haunt social media as a troll using fake avatars? Would he have a Twitter account bragging about his accomplishments? Would he be showcasing his wealth, his abs, his potential victims on Instagram? During Patrick's '80s reign, he still had the ability to hide, a possibility that simply doesn't exist in our fully exhibitionistic society. Because he wasn't so much a character to me as an emblem, an idea, I'd probably approach him again by addressing his greatest fear: What if no one was paying him any attention? Something that upsets Bateman terribly is that due to corporate-culture conformity, no one can really tell anybody else apart (and the novel asks what difference does it make anyway?). People are so lost in their narcissism that they're unable to distinguish one individual from another, which is why Patrick gets away with his crimes (even if they're in a fictional scenario). This also illuminates how few things have really changed in American life since the late '80s: they've just become more exaggerated, and more accepted. Patrick's obsession with his likes and dislikes and with detailing everything he owns, wears, eats, and watches has reached a new apotheosis. In many respects *American Psycho* is one man's ultimate series of selfies.

■ ■ ■

Christian Bale changed the look of Bateman for me, giving him a face, a spectacular body and a deep yet hesitant voice, noting that he took his cues from watching Tom Cruise on *The David Letterman Show:* what Bale called a very intense friendliness with nothing behind the eyes. He created an iconic portrayal, which can happen when you make a movie from a well-known text, whether it was Vivien Leigh as Scarlett O'Hara or James Mason as Humbert Humbert or Jack Nicholson as Jack Torrance; these actors get stuck in our heads, and we can never read the book again without picturing them—and those portraits tend to be frozen in time. But readers first came across Patrick Bateman near the end of my second novel, *The Rules of Attraction,* published four years before *American Psycho,* where he appears late one night in a Manhattan hospital in the waning days of 1985, waiting for his father to die. Sean, his brother and one of the novel's narrators, also comes to visit—begrudgingly, supposedly to pay his last respects, but really because he needs money—and he ends up getting dissed by the older brother he loathes. So Patrick Bateman started becoming real for me years before I started *American Psycho,* though I didn't have a clear sense of this at the time—which maybe is why I often find the question of where he might be now rather elusive. Bateman's so fixed for me in that particular time and place that I simply can't imagine him anywhere but in that lonely office at Pierce & Pierce, or committing his unfathomable crimes in that imaginary apartment on the Upper West Side, or lost and wasted in various trendy nightclubs.

Like many characters a writer creates, Patrick Bateman lives on without me, regardless of how close we became during the years I spent writing about him. Characters are often like children leaving home, going out into the uncaring world and being either accepted, ignored, extolled, criticized, no matter what the writer might hope for. I check in with him every now and then, but he's been on his own for years, and I rarely feel like his guardian or that I have any right to tell him where he should or shouldn't be living, decades after his birth—as if he'd listen to me anyway, much less care. The novel's twenty-fifth anniversary did, however, force me to look at how my character's considered now, compared to how people talked and thought about him in the months before the book was released. Some people who wanted the book banned then regarded Bateman's crimes (which might have been entirely imaginary thought crimes) as *my* crimes, a hideous mistake that contributed to the death threats I subsequently received, and to the censorship with which I was threatened. In 1991, this seemed like an unusual and curious response but these days people routinely mistake thoughts and opinions for *actual* crimes. Feelings aren't facts and opinions aren't crimes and aesthetics still count—and the reason I'm a writer is to present an *aesthetic*, things that are true without always having to be *factual* or immutable. But opinions can also change, even if, according to social media, they're supposed to be forever.

■ ■ ■

American Psycho: The Musical officially premiered in April 2016 at the Gerald Schoenfeld Theatre on Broadway, the fruition of a project that had been in the works for roughly a decade. I first heard about it in Los Angeles in either 2006 or 2007 at the Chateau Marmont when I had drinks with a group of young producers and managers, all male, all white, all straight, who were intent on bringing the book to the stage. I remember very little about that encounter since, in those hazy years, I was drinking heavily and distracted and lost in a midlife crisis so severe that I barely paid any attention to strangers during business meetings. But I do remember it was cocktail hour, the summer light was dimming, we sat at a table on the crowded patio, and everybody seemed so impossibly young and guardedly optimistic as we talked about a musical not based on the movie, but on my novel. The young men offered various vague reasons as to why they were interested: *American Psycho* had a brand that resonated, it was such a cool idea, it was an alternative to family-friendly Broadway fare, and maybe even straight dudes might buy tickets to a musical. They kept talking, and after another margarita I realized: these guys could have been anyone. But these were genuine fans, and they kept reiterating that this show could be very lucrative. They reminded me somewhat of the young men I'd met on Wall Street while I was uselessly researching this novel almost thirty years previously, except *I* was the older one now.

The entertainment business forces you to become a gambler whether you like it or not, and the young men were rolling the dice against odds that were decidedly not in their favor. Even if they did get the show to Broadway—that night at the Chateau there was no book for it, no music, no songs—the stark fact was that 80 percent of Broadway productions fail to recoup their costs. Yet, sure, it conceivably *could* be lucrative—and that sounded so nice, so hopeful, after a couple of drinks on the patio where I remember candles were being lit, and the garden was darkening—so why not let them try? At the very least I'd get some up-front option money. I kept nodding pleasantly that evening and asked only a few perfunctory questions whose answers I really didn't care about because I'd never get involved down the line. I just wanted everyone to be happy, confident that I was committed to their idea. Buzzed, I kept thinking, *Hey, this could be* lucrative.

■ ■ ■

It took many years for everyone to figure out their respective deals, and these emails and phone calls from agents and lawyers were my only reminders that people were trying to turn *Ameri-*

can Psycho into a musical. I was often involved in a myriad of other projects, and this idea still felt like such a long shot that it would evaporate from my mind the minute I got off the phone with an agent or a lawyer or a would-be producer. During that preproduction decade I had dinner only once, in 2010, with the writer of the musical's book, Roberto Aguirre-Sacasa, and it was strictly social: he already had his own take and didn't ask me any questions at all about the novel. I also met Duncan Sheik, who was writing the music and lyrics, once during that period, and then again, maybe a year later, at a cocktail party at the producer David Johnson's house in Brentwood. And I met Rupert Goold, the director of the production, one time at another dinner, and these dinners were civil and booked at expensive restaurants, and I drifted through each of them serenely since the whole idea seemed like a pipe dream. I always felt more than welcomed if also pleasurably useless—they were going forward with or without me, and I didn't care because I never thought it was going to happen, even if Duncan and Roberto and Rupert all had solid Broadway credentials. Jesse Singer, one of the show's producers, was my point person during the years of development, and he kept me up-to-date on everything that was and wasn't happening. But I had so many other distractions. For instance, getting used to being back in Los Angeles after twenty years away had proved harder than I anticipated; compared to Manhattan, it was a lonely town that bordered on the ghostly, and there was the movie version of *The Informers*, which had started out with so many good intentions but was turning into a creative and financial disaster, and I lost friends over it. I was meanwhile having a hellish time writing a new novel, which almost verged on memoir, detailing the midlife crisis that was burying me during that period. Finally, there was also the actor I'd fallen for, who was very interested in a movie role and committed to getting it—but nothing else, I found out the hard way.

■ ■ ■

Then suddenly it was December 2013 and *American Psycho: The Musical* was opening at the Almeida Theatre in London, with *Doctor Who*'s Matt Smith in the lead for a five-week run. This had happened so quickly that I was *amused* by how surprised I was, and how *strange* this notion felt, because it still didn't seem quite real. I'd heard the first demos that Sheik had made and sung himself, and I'd skimmed Roberto's book but just barely, since this project seemed light-years away from my practical life and day-to-day preoccupations: this was someone else's world. The producers offered to fly me to London for a week to do publicity, which I realized would not only make me the de facto face of the show but also might be misconstrued as my approval of a show I hadn't, in fact, seen. I wasn't in the mood to play a nice and grateful artist and I warned Jesse Singer that if they brought me over to walk the red carpet and talk to the press, I was going to be honest about whether I liked it or not. In the end they decided against the risk and the expense; besides, they didn't need any PR help since the entire run was sold out already. The Almeida production opened to good reviews, and there immediately was talk about moving the show to Broadway. Three years passed very quickly, and in the spring of 2016 I was flown to New York so I could see this staging in previews, immerse myself in a press junket, become the de facto godfather, and walk the red carpet and attend both premiere and the after party: my appearance sealing the deal that I approved of it all. And why wouldn't I? It could be *lucrative*.

The last time I had been in New York was in 2010, on the first stop of a book tour when I'd felt myself physically recoiling from the changes the city had gone through since I'd left five years before: more crowded, if that was possible, and more rich people; everything seemed cleaned up and slightly anonymous, as if globalization had waved its wand over Manhattan. The city in which I came of age during the late 1980s was so much dirtier, scarier and more thrilling than the corporatized and homogenized place I experienced during those few days on the book tour. Then, after completing a UK book tour and before doing another one in Australia, I was brought back to the city again to appear on the *Charlie Rose* show, and before that taping I spent an afternoon walking around kind of dazed at how different everything looked: calm and prosperous, safe for families, expensive and neutered, and so much less *crazy* than it had been in my twenties. And these feelings were amped up even further six years later, when the *American Psycho* musical opened on Broadway. By now this all seemed like an extremely long dream, and I could imagine what I would sound like if I were to describe it to anyone: a book I'd written had been turned into a musical and I had to fly to New York to watch it with a journalist from *The New York Times* sitting next to me and noting my reactions, and then I was backstage shaking hands with Bradley Cooper, and next we were both talking to Benjamin Walker, the star of the show, and then I was being interviewed at Sardi's and, later, at the 21 Club where a reporter from the *New York Post* ironically noted that I had ordered steak tartare, raw and chopped up and bloody red. But this wasn't a dream.

■ ■ ■

Even though the week was mostly devoted to the musical that we all hoped would be so lucrative, the other part of the trip happened to coincide with the upfronts—the beginnings of an advertising sales period—for Fullscreen, a digital company to which I'd sold a web series called *The Deleted* that I had written and would be directing later that summer. When I wasn't doing press for the musical, I was in my Midtown hotel room finishing up the remaining scripts or else taking an inventory at my apartment on Thirteenth Street, which I'd been renting out in a neighborhood I no longer recognized, or else hanging out with a few friends who had moved from Manhattan to Brooklyn and whom I hadn't seen in years. In the end, I didn't have to fake any PR niceties about *American Psycho: The Musical* because I genuinely liked the show, finding it problematic but enjoyable. Bateman's awareness that the society he's a part of doesn't care about his crimes and in turn forces him to imagine that maybe he didn't actually commit them, was a tricky thing to dramatize onstage; it's what had also proved difficult for Mary Harron in her adaptation for the screen, a failure to which she freely admits. An unreliable narrator might be best suited to the digressions of a novel, and all three times I watched the musical that week the second act always gave me pause, with a succession of scenes where Bateman is compelled to acknowledge his "truth" about himself and society. Overall, however, the material seemed more prescient than it ever had. In the wake of the distant economic collapse and the growing ascent of Donald Trump, it seemed as if this might just become the musical of the moment. As I watched Bateman rise before me one last time, I couldn't help but think back to that initial meeting at the Chateau Marmont a decade ago, where the summer light was dying and I was buzzed from a couple of cocktails, when I felt like this scheme might actually work out and be *lucrative.* In fact it closed two months later after eighty-one performances including a month of previews, at a cost of fourteen million dollars that was never recouped.

t h e s e d a y s

In the summer of 2018, I started watching a TV show that aired on Sunday nights, a sometimes riveting, sometimes moving, often frustrating series set in, of all places, the transgender ball-culture world in late-'80s Manhattan. Often, as I watched, I felt myself experiencing an actual physical reaction, whether it was an abrupt pang in the chest, a slight rush of adrenaline or a faint yet twitchy fearfulness, and I realized this was connected to the yearning for freedom that the main characters in this show all seemed to feel: a desire for acceptance, for their voices to be heard, to be included no matter what they represented or how repugnant they might seem to the status quo. It was a somewhat conventional prime-time soap, which seemed to take the characters' lives seriously, but their stories of pain and struggle took place in a world that didn't want to acknowledge them; because they were somehow *offensive* and so should instead be erased, invisible, banned, and this had, for me, in the summer of 2018, a stress-inducing timeliness that had nothing to do with the show itself.

The three trans women at the center of the show were resilient figures who could have been tragic given the unlucky moment they were born into, in which homophobia, AIDS and racism were rampant. But, at night, they had the ball-culture world, which allowed them to escape from the darkness of their real lives into an aspirational fantasy of freedom, where they competed for prizes, cat-walking and dancing down an imaginary runway of luxury, emulating other social classes and genders. At these balls the women were judged on voguing, costumes, appearance and exaggerated attitude, and their goal was to accentuate a parody of feminine heterosexuality. The characters' defiance here wasn't crushed by the real world, as it seemed to be almost daily in a place they wanted to fit into, but instead was judged by a panel that awarded them trophies based on their "realness," which was their *acting-out* fantasy version of themselves—avatars disguising themselves for a night of escape. This show was a reminder for me in the summer of 2018 that freedom was ultimately what everyone yearns for, no matter your age, your gender, your race, your identity. In the Manhattan of 1987 that I had resided in, freedom was a promise fulfilled only for certain people, and a particularly uneasy episode of the show reminded me of the now-obvious racism in the young, privileged, white-boy gay scene during that period, yet this strange and uneven series also reminded me of the shifting attitudes of what freedom, with all of its attendant limitations and illusions, meant *now*.

■ ■ ■

During that summer I had dinner with a friend who'd driven up from Manhattan Beach. I met him in Culver City after coming over from West Hollywood, a district that was still Resisting, actually going so far as to present a porn star who'd had a one-night stand with Donald Trump over a decade ago, and who'd been paid not to talk about it but had recently started giving interviews to humiliate him, with the keys to the city—instead of, say, to an advocacy group working for the homeless or even a *gay* male porn star. They were making a point, of course, but about what exactly seemed, like everything else in 2018, clouded by a particular brand of sentimental derangement. My friend and I hadn't seen each other in about a year, and we exclaimed about this before sitting down in a restaurant in the old Helms Bakery complex. We'd initially met when I moved back to LA in 2006, when he was working in Hollywood for a production company where a project of mine was being developed, growing somewhat miserable about the stark realities of the business. He's American, about a decade younger than me, and conservative. He'd voted for Trump and thought the president was doing a pretty good job, and sitting there with him I realized yet again that I was living with a Trump-hating millennial socialist and yet somehow that summer was able to go to the movies every weekend with a pro-Trump, pro-Israel, Jewish millennial, just as I could have drinks with a forty-year-old leftist journalist visiting from New York, or have dinner every month with a passionately anti-Trump liberal feminist in her fifties, just as I texted about bad TV shows weekly with a gay Jewish filmmaker in his thirties who supports Trump and on and on. So while sitting in that restaurant in Culver City I registered that my group of friends was politically *diverse*, and that even though I lived in blue-wave Los Angeles, I wasn't also living in a *political* bubble.

And neither was my friend from Manhattan Beach, though he admitted that over the last year easily half of his left-leaning friends had dumped him simply because he'd talked positively about the president on social media. The question for him now had become: Well, were any of them really his friends in the first place? If they could ditch him so completely over Trump, maybe they never had been. He'd often wondered: *Was this really all it took? Was defending the president you had supported and voted for that immoral and outrageous?* Apparently, for some on the Left this *was* reason enough to abandon a friend or a relative or even an acquaintance. My friend also noted that it was harder to meet girls online here in blue-state California, where it seemed "Where do you stand politically?" had become the question most frequently asked by females, replacing the previous: "How tall are you?" Like me, my friend accepted all ideologies and opinions, even those diametrically opposed to his own, and we noted how many of our friends *were* living in a bubble, still reeling over the "unfairness" of the election and the perceived evil of the Trump administration, and couldn't bear to consider a different view—that is, to stand in someone else's shoes. This was why it seemed to many of us in that summer that the Left was morphing into something it never had been in my lifetime: a morally superior, intolerant and authoritarian party that was out of touch and lacked any coherent ideology beyond its blanket refusal to credit an election in which someone they didn't approve of had, at least legally, technically, won the White House. The Left had become a rage machine, burning itself up: a melting blue bubble dissolving in on itself.

■ ■ ■

However, my friend and I were both well aware that we resided quite comfortably in what was now referred to as the bubble of white male privilege. Perhaps from certain angles this was true, but I didn't consider any of whiteness or maleness defining aspects of my identity—or at least hadn't been overly conscious of this (a fact, by the way, I can't do anything about). Still, along with millions of other white men, I was increasingly reminded by a certain faction, that we *should* be defining ourselves by our white identity because that was itself a real *problem*. Actually, this faction *demanded* it, without bothering to recognize that identity politics of any kind might be the worst idea in our culture right now, and certainly one that encourages the spread of separatist alt-right and all-white organizations. Across the board, identity politics endorse the concept that people are essentially tribal, and our differences are irreconcilable, which of course makes diversity and inclusion impossible. This is the toxic dead-end of identity politics; it's a trap. But even so I didn't reject people because they believed in this, or wanted to align themselves with a particular candidate. They were free to do as they wanted, and as a friend I supported them. I might not have agreed with them but I wasn't about to unfriend anyone because of what his politics happened to be. I'd never stopped hanging out with someone based on who he or she voted for, and maybe this was easier for me than for others because I just wasn't that interested in politics. Or else, as many would say, it was easier *because* I was a white privileged male. Or possibly because I'm simply a grown man, no longer a child, and understood that the world didn't always behave precisely as we wanted it to and also that people weren't all the same. I was far more interested in what people were really like, not who they voted for.

But in the summer of 2018 who you supported politically would determine if you were invited (or not) to a party or a dinner table or, as the White House press secretary learned one week that June, allowed to eat in a public restaurant. This had, for some of us, become an increasingly unacceptable form of "resistance"—something that after almost three years of Trump's ascendancy now felt stale, absurd, in bad faith. The shunning of others who don't think like you had moved past protest and resistance into childlike fascism, and it was becoming harder and harder to accept these exclusionary tactics. The differing political viewpoints were judged as immoral, racist and misogynist. This constant shrieking by the unconsoled was, for me, beyond tiresome, a high-pitched drone that never moved the needle. I figured that you might not like someone's politics or even his or her worldview but could still learn something useful and then move on. But if you look at everything only through the lens of your party or affiliation, and are capable of being in the same room only with people who think and vote like you, doesn't that make you somewhat uncurious and oversimplifying, passive-aggressive, locked into assuming you are riding the high moral tide, without ever wondering if you might not, in the eyes of others, be on the very bottom?

■ ■ ■

The summer hysteria of 2018 was never louder than when the future of the Supreme Court opened up, silencing my loudly unhinged boyfriend into a forty-eight-hour depression after Justice Kennedy announced his retirement, and friends started texting me in jacked-up despair, wondering what country they should move to. Add to this the supposedly *cosmic* immorality of the immigration policies now being enforced at the borders (Obama's were not *that* noticeably different), and the Resistance had officially become something different from what it started out as. It finally seemed time to close the door on this hysteria, a kind of fake game that didn't even come close to connecting with the real and the pragmatic, that by now felt manufactured and enacted and was almost never compelling or convincing—simply a desperate grab at, well, what exactly? Certainly not any notion of civility, or of accepting that the president was governing in a way that ninety percent of the people who'd voted for him *approved* of. Increasingly it looked as if there was an apparatus in play to delegitimize the election itself because some people simply hadn't gotten what they wanted. And Trump had forewarned them of this at all of his rallies, where "You Can't Always Get What You Want" consistently closed the show.

The country often felt like a demented high school where the losers in the student body were throwing everything they could at whoever had been elected class president just to see what might stick, at every turn undermining him as well as the students who'd voted for him. This was the dynamic, as I noted before, that kept turning Trump into the biggest underdog we've ever seen. The ongoing comparisons of him to Hitler, and of the Immigration and Customs Enforcement (ICE) to the Gestapo, was for me the last straw—after almost two years of the let's-wait-and-see-if-everyone-can-calm-the-fuck-down hiatus I'd maintained until the late summer of 2018, when *I* couldn't calm the fuck down anymore. And a new irony had entered the picture: I was now hearing about how irritating the Left had become from people *on* the Left. One evening over drinks someone sighed to me, "I don't know how we got so annoying." And at a dinner a middle-aged liberal scoffed, "Oh, I can't deal with the Resistance anymore"—and this from a gay man who'd been a proud member of it.

■ ■ ■

Walk away, I began hearing that summer. *Walk away, I'm just walking away. Just walk away.* This was a hash-tag I'd first noticed in the last week of June, and it was connected to young people who'd made videos that were posted on Facebook about why they were leaving the Democratic party. The founder of the #WalkAway Campaign was a young gay actor and ex-Democrat who'd grown disillusioned by the party's hectoring, inertia and bad faith, and after Hillary's debacle he'd had enough, as he believed many others had. "Once upon a time I was liberal. Well, to be honest, less than a year ago I was still a liberal," he announced in a video. "But I reject a system which allows an ambitious, misinformed, dogmatic group to suppress free speech, create false narratives and apathetically steamroll over the truth. I reject hate. These are the reasons why I became a liberal. And these are the same reasons why I am now walking away." This movement might have been small, but what made it seem larger was that it expressed something many people were talking about even before #WalkAway had become a campaign: the era of the traditional Democratic platform was dying, or actually had died in November 2016, or maybe even earlier, perhaps imploding somewhere along the road toward the shock of the election. It wasn't that Trump had won the Electoral College by so little, a disillusioned friend and Clinton supporter told me, it was that unfairness of the Electoral College over a dinner at Spago that cost thousands of dollars, and took Meryl Streep to task for her outraged anti-Trump speech at the Golden Globes the same week she'd put her Greenwich Village townhouse on the market for thirty million dollars. After that podcast aired I noticed a few acquaintances were no longer hanging out anymore, and that one or two people I actually considered friends had simply vanished—because, I supposed, I wasn't adamantly *against* the president, because I didn't agree with them that everything was *so god awful*, because I simply didn't think that Trump was the *worst thing to ever happen to democracy* and because it seemed to them I thought it was okay "orange Hitler" was in the White House. I was normalizing him, and that, comrade, was not acceptable.

I sometimes tweeted about how my virtue-signaling friends would lecture me, and on my podcast I talked about an LA-based producer's knee-jerk reaction when I mentioned a mutual acquaintance had voted for Trump and it looked as if she'd been bitten by a zombie out of *28 Days Later* and infected with the Rage virus. I made jokes like that not because I'd done anything to support whatever Trump had done, but only because I hadn't *clawed off my face in anguish* at something *he* had done, so they suddenly considered me a collaborator, and showed all the signs of this ghastly infection. Some of my podcast followers suggested that by complaining about leftist hysteria I was practically Rush Limbaugh incarnate, that I was an alt-right pro-Trump weirdo, that it was all garbage, it was disgusting, it was unbearable. And so here we were: the *opinion* of someone was *unbearable*. This was the stance now. And also an extreme, ludicrous violation of free speech, much as policies deemed unlikeable were misconstrued as immoral. The relentless Hitler and Nazi comparisons she'd lost it by *so much more* than anyone could've imagined, which was exactly why everyone felt so angry and unmoored, as if they'd been promised something so immutable that it was carved in stone. (My millennial partner was convinced that the #WalkAway Campaign was created and disseminated by Russian bots; it wasn't, but in the summer of 2018 who could really tell?) This campaign was a reaction against what many saw as an increasingly deranged and rabid resistance, which held that if you're not "woke" to how hateful and dangerous Donald Trump is, then you and his supporters should be subjected to an ever-widening social and professional fatwa. If you'd been cast out by your relatives, dropped by friends or lost jobs because you even *tolerated* this man, here were further indications that the Left was nowhere near as inclusive and diverse as long proclaimed. In the summer of 2018 they had turned into haters, helped by an inordinate amount of encouragement from the mainstream media, and now came across as anti-common-sense, anti-rational and anti-American.

■ ■ ■

Back in the spring of 2017 I'd lost a few friends (or false ones), not because I'd voted for Donald Trump (I hadn't) but because on my podcast I finally went off on wealthy coastal elites that were still sobbing about an election, and argued that this inability to rationalize and deal with a simple fact had become unbearable not only for them, but also for anyone who had to endure their theatrical trauma. I poked fun at rich friends growling about the were especially repugnant since my stepfather, a Polish Jew in his seventies, had as an infant, lost his family to the Holocaust, and I no longer could even *pretend* to sympathize with this hysteria; even as a metaphor, it was weak and basically moronic. However, my socialist boyfriend, whom I often accused of liberal fascism, now believed that my obsession with aesthetics had become, by the summer of 2018, essentially fascist as well.

■ ■ ■

Earlier that year, various journalists wanted to talk to me about a couple of tweets I'd posted in favor of Kanye West. They couldn't seem to believe that I supported his "crazy" feed, especially when he said he liked Trump, and couldn't fathom why I tweeted "Hail Kanye!" in response to his weird blend of transparent prophet and calculated PR prankster. There was the suggestion made by the press that there was something wrong with *me* for posting this, and not *them* in asking me why. But I'd known Kanye since 2013, when out of the blue he texted me to ask if I'd like to work on a movie idea of his. We'd never met, but I was intrigued enough to go see him in a private wing of Cedars Sinai the day after his first child had been born. We spent four hours there talking about the movie project and a wide range of subjects—everything from *Yeezus* to porn to *The Jetsons*—until Kim Kardashian came out of her room cradling their newborn North. This seemed the time for me to excuse myself, though it also seemed that Kanye wanted me to stay indefinitely, even offering me a Grey Goose that he was pouring out of a magnum as I prepared to leave. Since then

I'd worked with him on a few complicated and strange projects for film, TV and video that mostly never happened, yet because of all this I kept up with him on social media, and now found myself reacting to his amazing stream-of-conscious thoughts on his official Twitter page in the weeks before the release of his new record—just like hundreds of thousands of other followers.

These tweets were a reminder of why I liked Kanye: they were sweet and mysterious, dumb and profound, funny and playful, self-help speak and old pics, part absurdist stunt as well as a genuine reflection of where Kanye West was in that moment. And at one point during the twitter-storms he mentioned that he loved Trump, and admired his "dragon energy," which he suggested he and the president shared. But this admiration was nothing new, since he'd said as much when he imploded with a rant at a concert in San Jose the week after Trump won—and told the audience, "If I would've voted I would've voted for Trump." (My boyfriend was at that concert and almost had a meltdown.) On top of all this he was one of the only celebrities to visit the president in Trump Tower after the election. (Leonardo DiCaprio was another one but with a different mission.) All of this was pure Kanye, obsessed with showbiz and spectacle and power—and to some of us his honesty had always been hypnotizing and inspiring. But the Left acted like horrified schoolteachers, lecturing *us* that what *he'd* tweeted was very, very bad; that nobody should listen to him; that he should apologize so we all could forgive him for a narrative in which he—*a black man*—supported a racist and was therefore racist himself. In a moral panic, John Legend virtue-signaled at Kanye, and begged him to recant, recant, recant, and Kanye refused. As he did when *The New York Times*, even in an otherwise glowing profile in the Arts & Leisure section, couldn't process the Trump stuff either, and pushed Kanye to clarify and apologize, as if he needed to do so and, in his Kanye-like way, he refused.

■ ■ ■

What made tweets like "Self-victimization is a disease" or those in praise of the president so much fun was that they caused Trump's opponents to melt down even when they should've known better and taken these things in the spirit in which they were composed—as bi-polar, Dada performance art. But by taking Kanye so seriously, and literally, as if he were a Sunday morning pundit instead of a pop star, they twisted their meaning to fit a warped vision of the post-Trump world they'd imagined, a draconian, dystopian, 1984-meets-*The Handmaid's Tale* future. It almost became a game to play: What could one say that would upset them the most? But was it really fun—or just simply exhausting—to watch them go insane and get indignant about, well, just about anything? They had developed very precise rules about how to live and what opinions were allowed, about what made a person "bad" or "good" and which paths one could rightly follow, and Kanye West wasn't adhering to any of them. Instead of getting outraged all over again, they should have realized that a figure like Trump would seem appealing to him: brash, a gangster, his own man whether you liked him or loathed him, a loner, transparent, a truth teller not to be taken *literally*, flawed, contradictory, a rebel, awful for some or wonderful for others but certainly not vanilla or middle-of-the-road, incapable as a bureaucrat but skillful as a disruptor. This was also, of course, what a lot of other people I knew liked about Trump in the summer of 2018.

The media became derisive and speculated that Kanye had to be on drugs to say anything of the sort. He's *destroying his career!* How could a black man *like* Trump? And—shifting subjects, or targets—how could he promote Candace Owens? Owens, a young and pretty and compelling black woman, said she became a conservative when she finally understood that "liberals were actually the racists, liberals were actually the trolls." Owens was raised in Stamford, Connecticut and had worked at *Vogue*, and she had now become an activist in her own right, notably critical of Black Lives Matter. Owens asserted that Democrats were the real plantation owners, and at her college appearances she told young blacks to get over their self-victimization and identity-politics nonsense and stop comparing themselves to *actual* slaves. Kanye tried to make the same point in a rambling, faux-inspirational TMZ interview—along the lines of "slavery's all in your mind"—and the media began doubling down on their excoriation of all things and people somehow connected to him. Anyone but an idiot could tell what Kanye was *trying* to say, however garbled and clumsy it was, but given the bias infecting everything in 2018, the press worried that he was having "delusional episodes" and probably needed to be treated for drug abuse. Or maybe he'd just gone full-blown crazy, because no one who *wasn't* insane could ever think like this. The consensus, in postmortem editorials everywhere, was that he would never have a career again after the slavery comment and the Trump tweets. It was all over for Kanye.

■ ■ ■

I met up with Kanye during the week those controversies were exploding across social media, even though I hadn't initially wanted to. Kanye reached out because he was interested in resurrecting a TV project we had discussed in 2015, which he was now considering as a film. I was always intrigued by the basic idea but wasn't sure it would work as a movie, so I demurred, partly due to scheduling conflicts. He was soon heading to Wyoming to finish up production on his latest record, and in the interim it would be hard for me to find enough time for a meeting in his Calabasas offices. But then I realized that my hesitancy was colored somewhat by all that media coverage. I thought Kanye was probably okay, but maybe, like many were insisting, he *was* in some delusional or reckless phase, and if so, trying to get together in a week when I was already slammed with work and deadlines didn't make any sense. But when I explained that my schedule was problematic, he seemed disappointed, and in turn this disappointed me. So I promptly rearranged my schedule and made the drive out to his compound, flittingly apprehensive that I might be meeting, as the media kept reiterating, a man who'd lost his mind.

■ ■ ■

The year 2018 had been anxiety-inducing for a lot of people, many of them feeling like they were tumbling into free fall without a parachute. The Resistance seemed to be making a movie in which everyone was an actor and had a role and reading lines from a script, but it wasn't easy to tell if this was a horror picture or just another reality-TV series: What was real, and what wasn't? Everyone had a personal opinion, his or her own hot take on reality, and very few seemed to have the gift of neutrality, of being able to look at the world in a naturally calm, detached manner, from a distance, unencumbered by partisanship. Bias was everywhere. As an ironist I rarely got distracted—as happened above—by media spin, but if Sean Hannity on Fox presented a worldview that sometimes felt like a puffed-up fantasy aligning with the administration—and sometimes it didn't—then Rachel Maddow on the opposite side of the aisle at MSNBC, with her own labyrinth of arcane theories every bit as aligned to her audience's worldview, seemed pretty similar. Weren't they both, on one level, just smug partisan hacks? This divide was highlighted everywhere, and in one week that August I had two separate conversations with older women I knew, both in their seventies, both in the same socio-economic class, both white and college-educated, one from the East Coast and the other from the West. One of them told me that Trump frightened her so much she could barely think straight most days, while the other one told me that Trump was probably the greatest president of her lifetime. And each thought it was time to bring out a straitjacket for the other.

This anxiety wasn't confined only to politics and media. Ever since the election, Hollywood had revealed itself in countless ways as one of the most hypocritical capitalist enclaves in the world, with a preening surface attitude advocating progressivism, equality, inclusivity and diversity—except not when it came down to inclusivity and diversity of political thought and opinion and language. The passive-aggressive corporate hostility in play there was akin to that of a wrathful and deranged teenager, its attitudes and poses so childlike that you had to wonder if the fantasies the town peddled had engulfed logic and common sense completely. They proudly promoted peace just as they were fine with Trump getting shot by Snoop Dogg in a video or decapitated by Kathy Griffin or beaten up by Robert De Niro, or more simply, as an apparently drunken Johnny Depp suggested, assassinated. And the ominousness one felt wasn't restricted to the seemingly minor stuff, as when, in the summer of 2018, Whoopi Goldberg and Joy Behar on *The View* lost their shit over Trump and then cut off an invited guest who disagreed with them, and who was gone after the commercial break. There were more dangerous signs in the air.

■ ■ ■

Roseanne Barr's late-night tweet comparing Valerie Jarrett, a senior adviser of Obama, to a simian character in *Planet of the Apes* got her fired by the Walt Disney Company on the grounds of racism, even though Barr protested that she didn't even know Jarrett was black. This episode presaged Disney's other high-profile firing that summer of the writer-director James Gunn, who was responsible for the massively successful *Guardians of the Galaxy* franchise. Tweets from a decade ago had resurfaced, featuring tasteless bad-boy jokes, lame attempts at edgy low-brow shock humor that often touched on pedophilia, blowjobs, rape, AIDS. This was exactly what many of us thought Twitter had encouraged in its early years, back when "offensive" tweets didn't yet somehow define the entire humanity of an individual and land him in jail with a lifetime sentence. Disney severed all business ties with Gunn, whose movies had brought over a billion dollars to the corporation, and fired him off the next *Guardians* movie, which he'd already written and was scheduled to go into production that fall. What made this corporate decision so chilling was that Gunn had not only made amends for and disavowed these tweets years ago but was also an active hater of Donald Trump, loudly criticizing him on, naturally, Twitter. The realization hit that not even vehement liberalism could save you anymore, not in a tyrannical and oppressive Hollywood culture that was now dictating how we expressed ourselves as comedians, filmmakers, artists. Freedom of expression had become, it seemed, an aesthetic death wish, effectively suicidal.

With fewer and fewer corporations now running the show, (and soon it might just be one) fellow comrades might need to adhere to their new rulebook: about humor, about freedom of expression, about what's funny or offensive. Artists—or, in the local parlance, *creatives*—should no longer push any envelope, go to the dark side, explore taboos, make inappropriate jokes or offer contrarian opinions. We *could*, but not if we wanted to feed our families. This new policy required you to live in a world where one never got offended, where everyone was always nice and kind, where things were always spotless and sexless, preferably even genderless—and this is when I really started worrying, with enterprises professing control over not only what you say but your thoughts and impulses, even your dreams. Because of this enhanced corporate influence were audiences going to be able to consume material that was either unsanctioned or recklessly flirted with transgression, hostility, political incorrectness, marginality, the limits of forced diversity and inclusion, any kind of sexuality or anything at all that might be cursed with the now ubiquitous "trigger warning"? Were audiences willing to be brainwashed, or were they already there? How could artists flower in an environment while terrified about expressing themselves however they wanted to, or take big creative risks that often walked along the edges of good taste or even blasphemy, or simply those that allowed them to step into someone else's shoes without being accused of cultural appropriation? Take, for example, an actress getting shot down for a role she desperately wanted to have played—take a deep breath, comrade—*because she wasn't exactly that character already*. Weren't artists supposed to reside anywhere except in a risk-allergic safe-house where zero tolerance was the first and utmost requirement? This, at the end of the summer of 2018, seemed not only like an ugly intimation of the future but the nightmarish new world order. And the hyperbole I was accusing others of, I realized, I was now voicing myself—but I couldn't help it.

■ ■ ■

Kanye's behavior would continue to confound some people for months to come. In September, he would appear as a musical guest on *Saturday Night Live* wearing a Make America Great Again hat—the one Trump made famous during the 2016 election which had taken on, for both the Right and the Left, a kind of talismanic power that was either a symbol of racist-sexist red-state evil or, for believers, a symbol of patriotism and national pride. Wearing the hat had become, for some, an act of defiance—it could be dangerous and you could get into trouble, which is exactly why it became a fetish object Kanye loved, and said, in a meeting with the President at the White House a week later, that wearing the hat made him feel like Superman. He would top the *SNL* performance off with a free-associative rant where he would praise the President, dis a one-sided liberal media, accuse cast members of trying to bully him into not wearing the MAGA hat and essentially accuse leftists of being the real racists. And at the White House he talked to Trump about, among other things, prison reform, abolishing the 13th Amendment, and even a hydrogen-powered iPlane whose plans he was happy to share with his host, whom he would call the father he never had, and that he loved him very much and then ask if he could hug him. For this, Kanye was lambasted across the media landscape as a "token Negro" and "an attention whore" who should be "hospitalized" and that "what happened" to Kanye was "what happens when a Negro doesn't read books"—this actually coming from anchors on CNN and MSNBC—and this uneducated Negro bit became a talking point in the mainstream media that was still virulently anti-Trump. This is where the Left had ended up in the fall of 2018—and one darkly thought: *Maybe this approach would work for them, or maybe it wouldn't.*

Yet even in advance of these events, when I was driving up to Calabasas for the meeting I'd become apprehensive about, a fact was already crossing my mind, hard and immutable: the manic and rambling Kanye who had been freaking the media out in 2018 was, in fact, no different from the Kanye I'd met in the summer of 2013 in a wing of Cedars-Sinai or by the pool beneath a cabana at Kris Kardashian's house in Calabasas in 2014; this Kanye was no different from the man I'd hung out with in the Hollywood Hills when he was in the middle of recording *The Life of Pablo*, or wandered with him through his half-built house at the end of a cul-de-sac on a rainy afternoon before Christmas in 2015, where we'd watched *Cremaster 3* and he showed me a space that I thought was a closet but would actually become his wife's "glam" room. For that matter, this Kanye was no different than the performer I'd first seen at the Staples Center in 2008, when he went on a rant comparing himself to Jesus, John Lennon, Walt Disney, Elvis Presley and Steve Jobs. This ego and narcissism and grandiosity, the sheer insanity of his ambitions, and his dragon energy—it had *always* been on full display, but was now considered something new and tainted, redefined by the Resistance. Certain factions failed to recognize an artist who spoke in metaphor and poetry, who was often just funny and self-effacing, who you couldn't take literally—and *that* Kanye hadn't changed at all. But the now adamant opposition, both to him and what they believed he represented, certainly had. "You want the world to move forward?" Kanye would ask the SNL audience just a few weeks later. "Try love."

■ ■ ■

I arrived at Kanye's compound in Calabasas and after being ushered in by security, was brought into a room where he was multitasking: assembling the movie team, overseeing his fashion line, rehearsing new material. In the five years I'd casually known him, I'd never seen him so attentive and focused and happy. This was Kanye at his most lucid, and this afternoon confirmed for me that he was, in fact, sane: his own man, no apologies, and not some drugged-out freak gibbering on Twitter. People simply needed to acknowledge—not approve or to embrace—that here was someone who saw the world in his own way, and not according to how other people thought he *should* see it. What Kanye was championing in his Trump tweets was an idea of peace and unity, imagining a place where different sides could work together despite vicious ideological differences—that's it. He wasn't particularly interested in actual politics or literal policy, but it also seemed by the end of the summer of 2018 that no one else was, either. Kanye, like everyone else, on both sides of the divide, now envisioned the world as a theater where a musical was always playing, and hopefully starring someone like themselves voicing their own opinions. But in Kanye's case with the appropriate amount of narcissistic dragon energy, a power that allowed him, no matter what others thought, to be totally free.

■ ■ ■

What my friend and I were really discussing that night in Culver City—as disillusioned Gen X'ers who came of age during the one-two punch of the nihilistic '70s and the rah-rah Reagan '80s—was freedom. But how could you be free if you were bowing down to the shrieking antics on both sides of a Grand Canyon-size divide that no one was attempting to cross? Since November 2016 my friend and I had both heard that a horrendous economic collapse was about to materialize, the planet was going to melt, countless people would die, the fraught situation in North Korea would send the United States into a nuclear Armageddon, and

Trump would be impeached, brought down by a pee tape—leaving no jobs for anybody and Russian tanks in the streets. We also idly noted that the filmmaker David Lynch couldn't say *in an interview* that he thought *maybe* Donald Trump would go down as one of the great presidents in history, not without groupthink forcing him into apologizing for this immediately on Facebook. And where was a resistance that was so attractive and cunning that it managed to sway you, that maybe made you see things in a broader, less blinkered light? But the one we had in 2018 seemed bent on advocating mostly vandalism and violence. Trump's star on Hollywood Boulevard was destroyed with a pickax, an actor resembling a septuagenarian Lorax said "Fuck Trump" at the Tony Awards, a television hostess called the first daughter "a feckless cunt" on her TV program, another actor suggested the president's eleven-year-old son should be put in a cage with pedophiles. And all of this from Hollywood: the land of inclusion and diversity. Maybe nobody cared at all about Barron Trump, because this was simply the year of endless low points for a resistance that was spinning epic fails in venting their anger about Trump. Maybe it was just another episode in the reality show that is still unfolding. Or maybe when you're roiling in childish rage, the first thing you lose is judgment, and then comes common sense. And finally you lose your mind and along with that, your freedom.

A NOTE ABOUT THE AUTHOR

Bret Easton Ellis is the author of six novels, including *Less Than Zero* and *American Psycho*, and a collection of stories. He hosts *The Bret Easton Ellis Podcast*, available on Patreon. He lives in Los Angeles.

A NOTE ON THE TYPE

This book was set in Electra, a typeface designed in 1935 by William Addison Dwiggins (1880–1956). Electra cannot be classified as either "modern" or "old style." It is not based on any historical model, and hence does not echo any particular period or style of type design.

TYPESET BY NORTH MARKET STREET GRAPHICS, LANCASTER, PENNSYLVANIA

PRINTED AND BOUND BY BERRYVILLE GRAPHICS, BERRYVILLE, VIRGINIA

DESIGNED BY IRIS WEINSTEIN